THE
LAST BUFFALO

THE
LAST BUFFALO:

CULTURAL VIEWS OF THE PLAINS INDIANS:
THE SIOUX OR DAKOTA NATION

By

WILLARD E. ROSENFELT

Publishers

T. S. DENISON & COMPANY, INC.

Minneapolis

 T. S. DENISON & COMPANY, INC.

Standard Book Number: 513-01253-2
Library of Congress Card Number: 72-83234
Printed in the United States of America
by The Brings Press

Dedicated to:

My mother, Lois Rosenfelt
and
My uncle, C. D. Ommert

Preface

The following quotations are taken from an interview with Sitting Bull, by a New York Herald newsman in 1877, held at Fort Walsh, Northwest Territory.

NEWSMAN: ". . . will your people take up agriculture? Would any of them raise steers and go to farming?"

SITTING BULL: "I don't know."

NEWSMAN: "What will they do, then?"

SITTING BULL: "As long as there are buffaloes that is the way we will live."

NEWSMAN: "But the time will come when there will be no more buffaloes."

SITTING BULL: "Those are the words of an American . . . the buffaloes will not last very long . . . because the country there is poisoned with blood . . ."

Contents

APPENDIX

A Tribute to the Basic Philosophy of Some Courageous Sioux Leaders

Expressed simply but profoundly by the great Sioux leader Crazy Horse . . . "one does not sell (or give away) the earth upon which the people walk . . ."

Hetchetu aloh!

Photos and Credits

Little Crow—*courtesy of Minnesota Historical Society*

Sitting Bull —*courtesy of Minnesota Historical Society*

Gall —*courtesy of Minnesota Historical Society*

Kicking Bear —*courtesy of Minnesota Historical Society*

Rain in the Face —*courtesy of Minnesota Historical Society*

Red Cloud —*courtesy of Nebraska Historical Society*

Maps and illustrations by Howard Lindberg

Introductory Statement
The Dilemma of the Non-Indian World

The dilemma of the non-Indian world is that you or they—have lost respect for your mother—Mother Earth—from whom and where we have all come.

We all start out in this world as tiny seeds—no different than the trees, the flowers, the winged people or our animal brothers the deer, the bear or Tatanka—the buffalo. Every particle of our bodies comes from the good things Mother Earth has put forth.

This morning at breakfast we took from Mother Earth to live as we have done every day of our lives. But did we thank our Mother Earth for giving us the means to live? The old Indian did. When he drove his horse in near to a buffalo running at full speed across the prairie, he drew his bow string back and as he did so, he said, "Forgive me brother, but my people must live." After he butchered the buffalo, he would take the skull and face it to the setting sun as a thanksgiving and an acknowledgment that all things come from Mother Earth. He never took more than he needed. Today the buffalo is gone. Mother Earth is our real mother because every bit of us truly comes from her and daily she takes care of us. It is very late but still time to revive and rediscover the old American Indian value of respect for Mother Earth.

You say Ecology. We think the words Mother Earth have a deeper meaning. If we wish to survive, we must respect her. She is very beautiful and already she is showing us signs that she may punish us for not respecting her. Also, we must remember she has been placed in this universe by the one who is the all powerful, the great spirit above or Wakantanka—God. But a few hundred years ago, there lived in this land a people, the American Indian, who knew a respect and value system that enabled him to live here without having to migrate away from his Mother Earth in contrast to the white brother who migrated by the thousands from his Mother Earth because he had developed a different value system from the American Indian.

Carbon dating techniques say we were here for 30,000 to 80,000 years and that if we did migrate it was because of a natural phenomenon —a glacier—and not because of a social system that had a few rich controlling many, many poor, causing them to migrate as happened in Europe in 1500 to the present. We Indian people say we were always here.

We, the American Indian, had a way of living that enabled us to live within the great complete beauty that only the natural environment can provide. The Indian tribes had a common value system and a commonality of religion without religious animosity that preserved that great beauty that man definitely needs. Our four commandments from the Great Spirit are Respect for Mother Earth, Respect for the Great Spirit, Respect for Fellow Man (we are and will continue to be a nonprejudiced people) and Respect for Individual Freedom, provided that individual freedom does not threaten the people or the tribe or Mother Earth.

Our four sacred colors are red, yellow, black and white. They stand for the four directions—red for the east, yellow for the south, black for the west and white for the north. From the east comes the rising sun and new knowledge from a new day. From the south will come the warming south winds that will cause our mother to bring forth the good foods and grasses so that we may live. To the west where the sun goes down, the day will end and we will sleep and we will hold our spirit ceremonies at night from where we will communicate with the spirit world beyond. The sacred color is black and it stands for the deep intellect that we will receive from the spirit ceremonies. From the north will come the white winter snow that will cleanse Mother Earth and put her to sleep so that she may rest and store up energy to provide the beauty and bounty of springtime. We will also create through our arts and crafts during the long winter season.

All good things come from these sacred directions. These sacred directions or four sacred colors also stand for the four races of man—red, white, black and yellow men. We cannot be a prejudiced people because all men are brothers because all men have the same mother. You are my white sister and you are my white brother and you are my black brother and my black sister because we have the same mother—Mother Earth. He who is prejudiced and hates another because of his color hates what the Great Spirit has put here. He hates that which is holy and he will be punished even during this lifetime as man will be punished for violating Mother Earth. This is what we Indian people truly believe.

We the Indian people, also believe that the red man was placed in America by the Great Spirit and the white man in Europe and the black man in Africa and the yellow man in Asia. What about the brown man? The brown man evolved from the sacred colors coming together. Look at our Mother Earth. She, too, is brown because the four directions have come together. After the Great Spirit, Wakantanka, placed them in their respective areas, he appeared to them in a different manner and taught them ways so that they might live in harmony and true beauty. Some men, some tribes, some nations have still retained the teachings of the Great Spirit. Others have not. (This no doubt shocks those who came upon our people to destroy our religious beliefs and who had the stereotype that we Indian people are pagans, savages or heathens, but we do not believe that only one religion controls the way to the spirit world that lies beyond.) We believe that the Great Spirit loves all his children equally although he must be disturbed at times with those of his children who have raped and pillaged Mother Earth because they worshipped gold or green as their sacred colors and placed materialistic acquisitions as their God even to the point of enslaving their fellow man so that they may own and possess more material goods.

Brothers and sisters, we must go back to some of the old ways if we are ever going to truly save our Mother Earth and bring back the natural beauty that every man seriously needs especially in this day of drugs, tranquilizers, insane asylums, ulcers, extreme poor, extreme rich who share nothing, prisons, jails, rigid boundaries, and complete annihilation weapons.

A great Hunkpapa Sioux Chief, Sitting Bull, said to the Indian people, "Take the best of the white man's road, pick it up and take it with you. That which is bad leave it alone, cast it away. Take the best of the old Indian ways—aways keep them. They have been proven for thousands of years. Do not let them die."

My friends, I will never cease being an Indian. I will never cease respecting the old Indian values especially our four cardinal commandments and values of generosity and sharing. I believe that the white man became so greedy that he destroyed many things. I also believe that the white man has done a great deal of good in this world. He has good ways and he has bad ways. The good way of the white man's road I am going to keep. The very fact that we can all speak freely, the very fact that we talk a common language and can still exchange knowledge, the fact that we can exchange knowledge immediately over a wire to another country, shows the wisdom of my white brothers. These ways I will always keep and cherish, but my white brothers, I say you must give up this materialism to excess. Keep those material goods that you need to exist. Be more of a sharing and a generous type person. Have more respect for aged and the family tradition. Have more respect for an extended family which extends not only from mother and father and son and daughter but goes on to grandmothers and grandfathers and aunts and uncles—goes out to the animal world as your brother, to Mother Earth and Father Sky and then above to Tankashilah, the Grandfather, Tankashilah means Grandfather. Wakantanka means the Great Spirit. They are both the same. When we pray directly to God, we say Tankashilah because we are so family-minded that we think of Him as our Grandfather and we are his grandchildren. And, of course, Mother Earth is our mother because Grandfather intended it so. This is a part of the great deep feeling and psychology that we have as Indian people. It is why we preserved and respected our ecological environment for such a long period.

Only with the thought that Mother Earth is truly a holy being and that all things in this world are holy and must not be violated and that we must share and be generous with one another—only with this thought —you may tell it in your fancy words as psychology, theology, sociology or philosophy—call it whatever way you wish but think of Mother Earth as a living being. Think of your fellow man as a holy person who was put here by the Great Spirit being, of the four sacred colors and think of brown also as a sacred color. With this philosophy in mind, as you go on with your environmental ecology programs, you will be far more successful as a nation when you truly understand the Indians' respect for Mother Earth.

ED McGAA, Oglala Sioux

Acknowledgment

The author wishes to express his most sincere appreciation to his friend Ed McGaa, Oglala Sioux, former Executive Director of the Upper Midwest American Indian Center, and presently Assistant City Attorney in St. Paul, Minnesota, for permission to use his remarks in the foregoing introduction. Mr. McGaa was most helpful in evaluating this manuscript and his advice, especially in the area of religion, has been of immeasurable value.

The author fully realizes that any attempt to convey the rich cultural heritage of a people might fall short of perfection, but with the conviction that the Sioux culture represents one of the world's greatest civilizations, an honest attempt has been made to present this book for the general reader's appreciation.

The greatest treasure the American people have yet to discover is the deep culture of the American Indian. It is not impossible to adopt aspects of the Indian's cultural life style for a richer, more enjoyable modern-day life style.

This book does not deal in great depth with aspects of the Sioux culture, rather it has been intended to provide opportunity for readers to look beneath the surface at many cultural aspects and to reshape thought and stereotype impressions that might have previously been falsely represented through various white oriented media.

It is a beginning.

Dakota (Sioux) Tribal Names

The Dakota people all spoke the same language originally, but as the tribes became scattered, each of the divisions used its own form of the language.

The Eastern division retained the original name of Dakota. The Middle division called themselves Nakota while the Western or Teton tribes referred to themselves as Lakota. All three major groups were of the same Dakota nation.

EASTERN DAKOTA (Santee)

1. Mdewakanton
2. Wahpeton
3. Wahpekute
4. Sisseton

MIDDLE DAKOTA

Yankton and Yanktonai

WESTERN DAKOTA (Teton)

1. Blackfoot
2. Two Kettle
3. Miniconjou
4. Hunkpapa
5. Brule
6. Sansarc
7. Oglala

The map below shows the migration routes of the various divisions of the Dakota as they moved gradually from their woodland environment onto the plains.

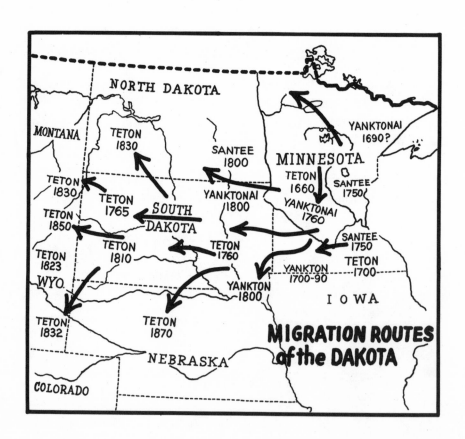

MIGRATION ROUTES of the DAKOTA

The Plains Indian

The Sioux (Dakota) people had what our present world seems to have lost, and what has been lost must be regained. Their reverence for the human personality, together with their respect for the earth and its web of life were at the center of their culture and all things revolved around this philosophy. They had a world view and a self view that no society before or since has surpassed. This outlook provided both tradition and institution and was an art to be ranked supreme among the arts known to mankind.

If our present-day society should be able to recapture this power, the earth's natural resources and ecological balance would not be in danger of being lost forever as they appear to be now.

These people could neither read nor write in terms of the white man's culture, and thus were told in many ways that all they believed in and cared for, had to die. For years the social destruction that was thrust upon this proud people took its toll. The white society eventually came to believe that this group of people had given up its tradition and values, and was on the trash heap of our social order. That they should be taken care of as part of a welfare state it was agreed, since pangs of guilt were evident in many bosoms.

The white conqueror, for reasons military, economic and religious, pronounced the death sentence on these people many years (and tears) ago. Through legal means, administrative order and military slaughter, this group was nearly wiped from the earth. Through slavery, forced dispersal, elimination of food supply, forced migration, and attempted religious conversion, they were driven to the brink of oblivion. Through contact with the onrush of a new society, with which they attempted to exist peacefully, they were decimated by the white man's diseases, tricked by the white man's treaties, and saw their values trampled under the feet of a society that did not understand them, nor indeed want to understand them. They were viewed with scorn because they were different, and viewed as hostile since their leaders saw fit to defend their land and their culture. Their leadership was destroyed through killing of the body and through killing of the soul. Leaders were bribed, replaced, and otherwise manipulated to conform with the views of an expanding frontier society. Their very lives became pawns in the deadly game of national politics, a game in which they provided the yardstick in which to measure the popularity of military heroes, some of whom had designs on the presidency of the nation. The rules of the game were to kill. Kill by any means and the more killed the more popularity for some military leaders.

To many tribes this death hunt brought total destruction. To others it brought mortal wounds, but to some it brought a vow to preserve those things held dear. The language, religion, culture system, symbolism and attitude toward nature, man and universe, although pounded unmercifully, lived on in the hearts of the survivors. It is there today, living perhaps as a tree in the desert, but living. Perhaps the sacred hoop will again be made intact. Perhaps the flowering tree of their nation will again bloom. If this happens, then the descendants of this group may again lift up their heads and demonstrate the values and philosophies that were the fundamentals of their existence. Perhaps these qualities may be shared with other groups, and perhaps all groups can live together, each the richer for the experience.

DAKOTA
CULTURES

The Horse in Dakota Culture

The Dakota were not always plains dwellers. Long before the white man came, they lived in or near the forests and lived off the bounties of the forest and the waters. Little by little they were pushed from the north country and onto the plains by their enemies. Here they adapted to the environment and became hunters. The buffalo had become a principal food source even before the horse was available to them.

When the Spanish came into the Southwest, they brought horses to a land in which there was none. Many of these escaped and over the years multiplied into large herds. From this source and through stealing from their enemies, the Dakota people accumulated vast numbers of the animals and utilized them in many ways.

All the Plains Indians taught their children that to steal horses from one's enemy was an act of bravery and of much importance, for if the enemy was relieved of his horses his ability to wage war was lessened.

Horses became a symbol of wealth to the Dakota, and a warrior's wealth was determined by the number of horses he had. Marriages were determined by how many horses the prospective husband could pay to the young lady's parents, and the more horses paid for the marriage, the higher the young lady was thought of in Dakota social circles.

The horse was used in hunting buffalo and, since it could run faster than the buffalo, the opportunity to secure food became much easier.

Horses were also used to drag the "travois" or polelike structures, on which belongings were carried from one camp to another, and enabled the tribes to roam great distances over the prairies in search of buffalo.

25

Travois

They also provided a means of escaping swiftly from approaching enemies and provided a means of conducting war raids. The mounted warriors were able to attack and retreat swiftly as the occasion demanded. The Dakota became skillful horsemen and to many became known as the "Horse Indians."

Buffalo: The Dakota Staff of Life

The Dakota tribes over a period of time became plains dwellers and had no permanent villages or towns. They moved their homes (tepees) from place to place, usually in their search for food. They became very dependent on the buffalo as their main source of food, and for this reason the buffalo hunt took on great meaning to them.

Each tribe or band had special scouts who ranged far and wide to discover buffalo herds. When they reported a discovery to the band, elaborate plans were made for the hunt. The hunt was in complete control of one of the warrior societies (akacitas) of the tribe. Special police guards were sent out to protect the herd until all hunters were ready. Anyone found breaking the rules of the hunt, by attacking too soon, or going ahead of the hunt warriors, was severely punished. When the signal for attack was given, it was every hunter for himself. Whoever killed a buffalo could keep it for his own family's use.

After the hunt, the women of the tribe took the meat and dried and preserved it for food to be used during times of scarcity. The skins of the buffalo were carefully scraped and cleaned, then dried and treated so that they were soft and pliable. These skins were used for clothing, robes, and tepee covers. Bones of the animals were often used to make tools for the family. The large rib bones were sometimes tied together and used by the children as toboggans in winter. Strips of the hide, not cured (rawhide), were used in making ropes, saddles, food bags, and soles for moccasins. Often the horns of these animals ended up as part of a headdress or warbonnet for the great men of the tribe.

After a successful hunt, the tribe would have a huge feast on the good, fresh meat. That meat remaining after the appetites had been satisfied,

27

Scraping a Buffalo Hide

Making Pemmican

was made into "pemmican," which could be kept for long periods of time without spoiling. To make pemmican, the dried meat was pounded into bits and stirred into a mixture of hot tallow (buffalo fat). Sometimes wild berries were pounded into the mixture, and this delicacy was called "wasna." It was then poured into rawhide bags called "parfleches" or sometimes the tough intestines of the buffalo, and tied shut for future use.

The Dakota had a variety of hunt plans and it was the responsibility of the warrior society in charge of the hunt to decide on which plan to use. One way was by stalking, done by individual hunters. These hunters would often disguise themselves with a wolf skin and try to get close enough to the animals for a shot, either with bow and arrow or rifle.

Another method in popular use, when many buffalo were needed, was to build a corral at the foot of a cliff. Above the cliff, two long lines of rock piles were arranged. Warriors would hide behind these rock piles and as the medicine man lured the animals between these lines, the men would rise up as needed and wave blankets, causing the buffalo to stampede between them. In their panic, the shortsighted animals would tumble over the cliff into the enclosure below. Hunters waiting below would then finish killing the crippled animals.

In level terrain, where cliffs were not convenient, other methods were used. One was to surround a herd with grass fire and then advance around the panicked animals, shooting as many as possible. Still another method was to stampede a herd so that it might run between two waiting lines of hunters, who would shoot them as they passed.

Still another method which called for great skill was for the mounted hunters to race alongside the running buffalo and shoot them as they rode.

All methods worked well for the Dakota, and they managed to base their existence on the success of the hunts.

It is important to note that these people killed only enough buffalo to satisfy their needs. They were practicing a form of conservation that would preserve their food supply for many years to come.

The coming of the white man changed all this. As railroads were built through the Dakota hunting lands, marksmen were hired to kill the buffalo, as they created a danger to the trains. Thousands upon thousands of these animals were slaughtered and left to rot where they fell. Other white hunters came into the area and killed buffalo to get the skins which they would sell for a profit to Eastern markets. These buffalo hunters usually let the meat go to waste. Still other white men would shoot the buffalo just for the sport of killing.

Soon, the vast herds of buffalo began to disappear and with their disappearance the plight of the Dakota people became very serious. Their food supply was being taken away from them even though some treaties with the white government had guaranteed to leave the buffalo and the hunting grounds alone. Understanding the plight and concern of the Dakota nation over this situation, it is much easier to understand why they decided in many cases to fight for what they thought was theirs. The hope of the Dakota nation was snuffed out along with the senseless killing of the buffalo.

Many years later, the following historic site marker was placed by the roadside not far from where the historic battle of the Little Bighorn occurred:

BUFFALO COUNTRY

Buffalo meant life to the Plains Indians and the mountain Indians used to slip down from the hills for their share, too. Some tribes would toll buffalo into a concealed corral and then down them. Another system was to stampede a herd over a cliff, but the sporting way was to use bows and arrows and ride them down on a trained buffalo horse. Fat cow was the choice meat. The Indians preserved their meat long before the whites ever had any embalmed beef scandals. They made pemmican by drying and pulverizing the meat, pouring marrow bone grease and oil over it and packing it away in skin bags. It kept indefinitely and in food value one pound was worth ten of fresh meat. Tanned robes and rawhide were used for bedding, tepees, clothes, war shields, stretchers, travois, canoes, and bags. Horns and bones made tools and utensils. The buffalo played a prominent part in many of their religious rites and jealousy of hereditary hunting grounds brought on most of the intertribal wars.

It might be added to this inscription that the buffalo directly or indirectly led to the wars between the U. S. Army and the Dakota nation. If the white man's government had spared these animals and preserved the Indian hunting grounds, as they promised in their treaties, the historic battle of the Little Bighorn might never have been fought.

Horn Spoon

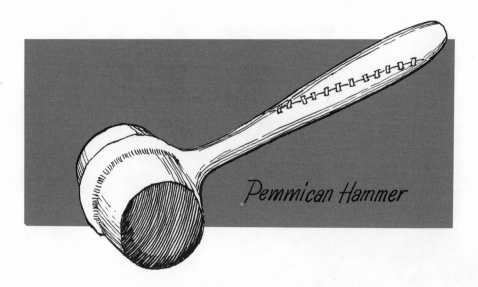

Pemmican Hammer

Food and Cooking

The buffalo hunt provided fresh meat for the tribe and everyone literally ate until their appetites were satisfied. The meat that was left was then cut up into strips, dried and smoked for future use.

The buffalo were skinned and cut up where they fell, and the hunter who made the kill was entitled to keep the choice cuts of meat as well as the skin. The rest was usually made available to anyone who needed meat.

Horns and many bones were removed and cleaned for use in making tools and other utensils. The fat was kept in skin bags, to be used in the making of "pemmican" or "wasna." The product kept indefinitely and sustained the people in the months when food became scarce.

Raw buffalo liver was a prized delicacy to the Dakota and was usually the first meat to be eaten after the hunt.

Meat was cooked either on a stick or by a method of stone boiling. Meat and water would be placed in rawhide bags and hot stones dropped into the bag at intervals until the water became hot enough to cook the meat. Sometimes the stomach of the buffalo was used as a cooking container. Firewood was often hard to find, especially on the open prairies, and in this circumstance dried buffalo chips were used for fuel. They burned with very little smoke and produced a very hot flame.

Wild berries, wild turnips, and other roots were also used as a source of food. Other wild animals such as the deer and elk were also objects of the hunter's search. Waterfowl and fish were also a part of the diet when they could be obtained.

The Dakota knew their environment very well, and learned to live by wise use of the foods that nature provided.

35

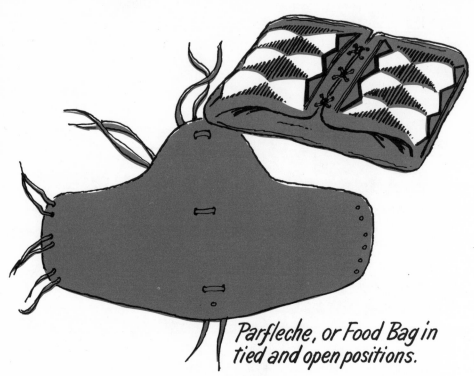

Parfleche, or Food Bag in tied and open positions.

Stone Boiling

Clothing

The Dakota people utilized the bounties of nature to provide clothing for the family. Normal attire for the men and boys was usually a skin "breechcloth," and moccasins. Sometimes leggings were worn. These were made from skins and fringed and decorated to suit their fancy.

In wintertime, the moccasins were stuffed with grass or hair for insulation, and a buffalo robe, worn hair-side in, offered some protection against the cold. These robes were decorated by the women, but sometimes the man would paint pictures of his brave deeds or accomplishments on it. A shirt made from deer or elk skin was also worn, and these were beautifully decorated with beads, quills, feathers, and polished bone.

The women and girls wore moccasins, short leggings and dresses made from elk skins, fringed with buckskin streamers. Beads and quills were woven artistically onto these garments into beautiful geometric designs, and often elk teeth were worn as ornaments. The Dakota women were famous for their skills in making and decorating clothing.

In the construction of moccasins it is interesting to note that the Dakota people curved the soles of the moccasins to conform to the left and right foot, while white pioneers were still wearing shoes that were designed the same for both feet.

Sioux Man's Clothing

Sioux Girl's Dress
ornamented with elk teeth.

Woman's
Tanned Skin Dress

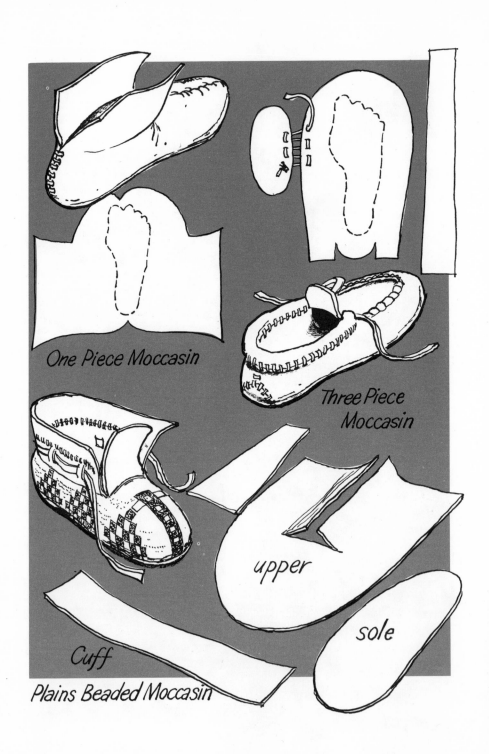

One Piece Moccasin

Three Piece Moccasin

Plains Beaded Moccasin

Cuff

upper

sole

The Tepee

The tepee was the Dakota version of the mobile home of their day. It was cool in summer and warm in winter. It was a structure supported by sixteen to twenty poles, each about twenty feet long. These poles were either cedar or pine which were stripped and seasoned. Most of the Dakota tribes usually made an annual trip into the Black Hills to replenish their pole supply since these trees grew in abundance there.

In making a tepee, the tops of three poles were lashed together by rawhide strips and set up as a sort of tripod. These were anchored to a ground pole or stake inside the tepee. The rest of the poles were leaned against this tripod, forming a circular base at the bottom, and then tied in place. This framework was then covered with twenty or more buffalo hides, sewed together, and stretched tightly around the frame. These homes could be set up in just a few minutes and, when necessary, could be taken down and made ready for travel in an equally short time.

The door of the tepee was an oval opening about one foot off the ground and had a removable cover that could be closed, much as a door. The tepee was usually set up with the door or opening facing east, away from the prevailing winds. Smoke wings or openings were located near the top of the framework, and regulated both draft and smoke removal by opening or closing.

Inside the tepee, a lining of skins was fastened all around the walls. This lining protected against drafts and rain water. In winter, grass was stuffed between these two layers, giving more insulation.

The women decorated the interior walls or skins, and the men would decorate the outside with pictures showing their deeds or exploits, or with some other characteristic of the family or tribe.

Tepee Interior

Inside the tepee the firepit or cooking area was located just back of the center area. Beds or sleeping robes were located around the walls. The mother would usually sleep near the door, and the father near the rear of the tepee with the children scattered around the rest of the circular wall area. Beds consisted mainly of grass padding covered with buffalo robes and skins. A back rest of willow sticks was built at one end of each bed, for these were used for sitting as well as for sleeping. Personal belongings, food and other items were either stored in pits, or tied and suspended from the lodgepoles.

The tepee was more than just a tent, it was a carefully engineered home, designed with many purposes in mind. It served the Dakota people well, and made their "mobile home" life far more comfortable than one might think.

Marriage, Family and Children

Each Dakota family was able to take care of its own needs. They traveled in bands or groups of families, but each family took care of its own food supply, its clothing and its part of the horse herd. Families and relatives were very close and felt strong ties between them. Uncles, aunts, cousins, grandparents all were loved and respected by the members of the families. These relatives often came to each other's aid in times when one family needed food, clothing or horses.

Often a young man might not have enough horses to give for his bride, and in these cases the relatives would usually contribute to the fund. The young couple was given a new tepee by the relatives, as well as many furnishings needed to set up housekeeping. When a baby was born, the relatives gave many gifts of clothing to the young family.

In the Dakota society, the custom of sharing was always observed. When food was plentiful everyone had enough to eat, and when food was scarce, it was given first to the very old and the very young, and often the rest went hungry. Should anyone be homeless or in need, he was taken in by other families and provided for. The Dakota people realized that they all must work and share together if the tribe were to survive. This lesson, while simple and easy to understand, has never been mastered by many of the white societies of the world.

Children were the center of love and attention, yet they were never kissed in public. They were rarely punished, and spanking was unheard of. The Dakota children were brought up in a society where they learned their responsibilities quite early in life and their respect for parents and older people was a part of their belief.

Sioux Baby in Cradleboard

Babies were not allowed to cry, and were always picked up and soothed before crying became a habit. It is possible that the Dakota parents did not want to disturb their neighbors, and, of course, a baby's cry might be heard by an enemy, resulting in tragic consequences.

The Dakota had no schools as we know them, but they did take great pride in the education of their children. The lessons that were taught were those that would prepare the children to live a productive life in the tribe.

The training of the boys was usually taken over by members of the warrior societies, quite often an uncle or other relative. They were taught

Teaching Tribal Traditions

the skills of horsemanship, archery, hunting and horse stealing. Now when we speak of horse stealing, we must look at this act in light of how the Plains Indian culture regarded it, not as the white man's culture saw it. To the Plains Indians, the horse was a thing of great value, and to take horses from an enemy not only made the warrior wealthy, but it deprived the enemy of his means of making war. Thus, it was considered a very valuable act and required a great deal of bravery on the part of a warrior to go into an enemy camp and get away with horses. Boys were also taught to endure many things, pain, hunger and exposure to weather elements,

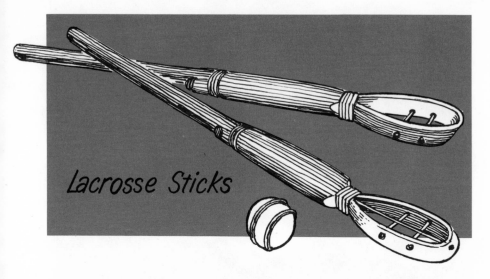

Lacrosse Sticks

for all these traits would be necessary in the years ahead. Bravery was a highly respected quality among the Dakota, and there was no place for cowards in a warrior society.

The girls were taught the jobs and duties of the tepee. They must learn how to cook and to prepare food. They must learn how to scrape and clean buffalo hides and other animal skins and how to make these articles into robes, clothing, and tepee coverings. They must also learn the crafts, such as weaving and clothing decoration.

Tribal conditions and sacred or religious matters were usually taught to the young by the older, wiser members of the family, and these were taught in such a way that the youngsters held them to be perhaps the most important lessons in their lives. Their respect for tribal traditions and their reverent respect for nature and its contributions to their lives were examples that other societies of the world would do well to study.

Since the horse was an important part of the Dakota life, it was necessary that all warriors be skilled in horsemanship. Saddles were for women. The warriors needed only a folded blanket with a girth strap, and a rope halter, with no bit in the horse's mouth. They mounted their horses from the right side and learned to ride almost from the day they were big enough to get on the horse. Each warrior usually had many horses, since they were considered wealth and prestige items in the tribe. Some horses

The Hoop and Pole Game

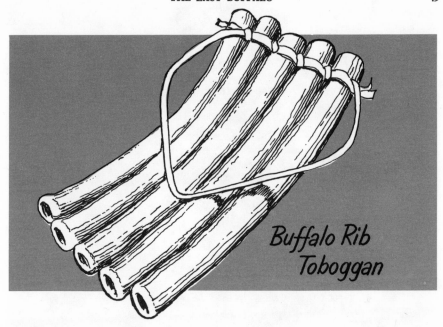

Buffalo Rib Toboggan

were trained to run alongside the buffalo so that the rider might shoot while traveling at great speed.

The Dakota people enjoyed games and recreation as well as anyone. They were fond of storytelling sessions, and had several games that involved objects similar to what we might call dice throwing. They were quite fond of foot-racing matches, and many a young warrior gained prestige for his fleetness of foot. Horse racing was another favorite sporting event, as were sharpshooting contests with either bows and arrows or later with rifles. Other games enjoyed were lacrosse, a forerunner of modern-day football, and a game called hoop and pole. A disclike object would be hurled into the air and the participants would throw a spearlike stick at it, attempting to spear it in flight. Tobogganing was popular with the Dakota youngsters. Their toboggans were usually made by tying several buffalo ribs together.

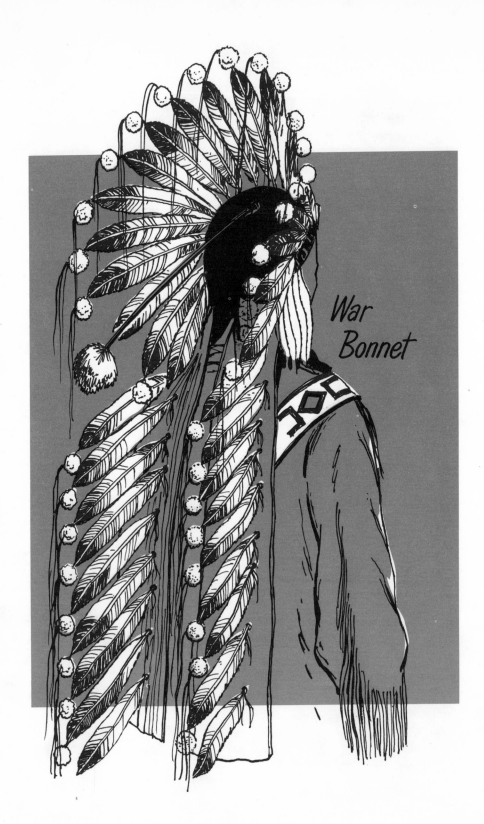

War
Bonnet

Warfare

War to the Dakota was a kind of game in which there were rules and points to be gained. There was personal glory to be gained by the individual warrior. He was admired for risking his life, and highly respected for the number of enemy scalps taken in battle.

Horse stealing was often a part of war, and here, too, the successful warrior gained great glory in the tribe.

While engaged in battle, the Dakota would make every attempt to gain what we might call honor points by striking an enemy with a "coup" stick or with anything he had available to strike with at the moment. Striking a live enemy first was worth more points than striking a dead enemy, and those warriors striking second, third, or fourth naturally did not earn the "coups" that the first warrior on the scene would.

The killing of an enemy was also a part of the honor award system, and eagle feathers, worn to signify these deeds, were awarded by the tribal council. One who didn't rate a feather was not permitted to marry until he was twenty-five years of age. Many battles were followed by council gatherings in which each warrior proudly reenacted his coups for the benefit of the group.

Dakota warriors applied war paint to their faces and bodies before entering a battle. The markings were used to signify their own deeds or to adhere to some object or meaning that they had seen in a dream or vision. These markings were often thought of as making the warrior more invincible to his enemy. They also carried sacred bundles, a bag of objects each of which had religious meaning to the warrior and which might add strength or invincibility in battle.

51

Sioux War Shield and Bow and Arrow

Weapons used in war were the bows and arrows, rifles, lances, war clubs and hatchets or tomahawks. Each warrior also carried a knife, and when possible a pistol was a prized weapon to take into battle.

Each warrior had a battle shield, decorated with "medicine" or secret power designs related to his dreams or visions. The power of this "medicine" was thought to work against those enemies who looked upon it. Often in battle the large shield was a burden to carry and many would make smaller replicas of the shield to carry into battle, not to stop enemy arrows, but to work his medicine for him.

To the Dakota warrior, death was honorable, and to give one's life in fighting for his people was the expected role of a warrior society member.

The Dakota tribes are perhaps the best known of all Indian tribes with regard to bravery and war, but despite all the movies that have been made depicting them as a warlike people, they usually did not fight a war or series of battles unless they were defending their land or their people.

The Circle in Dakota Culture

The circle has long been a very important symbol in the Dakota (Sioux) culture. This symbol was an important part of their religious belief and played an important part in the affairs of daily living.

The Dakota believed that the power of the world or universe worked in circles. The sky was round. Stars were thought to be round. The wind whirled in circles. Birds made their nests using the circle as a part of their architectural plan. The sun came up and went down in a circular path across the sky. The moon followed a similar circular path across the heavens. Both the sun and the moon were round. The seasons of the year seemed to follow a circle, always returning to where they were. Tepees were built with a circular base and were set up usually in half or full circles in encampments.

It was believed that human life traveled in a circular path from birth to death. As Black Elk reasoned, ". . . is not the South the source of life and does not the flowering stick (Sioux nation) come from there? And does not man advance from there toward the setting sun of life? Then does he not approach the colder North where the white hairs are? And does he not arrive, if he lives, at the source of light and understanding, which is the East? Then does he not return to where he began, to his second childhood, there to give back his life to all life, and his flesh to the earth from whence it came? The more you think this the more meaning you will see in it."*

It was believed that the woman was the life of the flowering stick or tree (Sioux nation), and the man must feed and care for it. When the

*From *Black Elk Speaks*, by Neihardt, University of Nebraska Press, pages 203-204, 1961. Permission of University of Nebraska Press.

nation's hoop (circle) was broken, there was no longer a center for the flowering tree to bloom and prosper.

In battle, the Sioux sometimes attacked their enemies by riding around them in circular fashion, firing and narrowing the circle as the fight progressed. On some occasions they made use of two attack circles with riders in the two circles traveling in opposite directions.

Many of the Sioux dances also made use of the circle in their religious applications.

Many historic records indicate that the forced life on reservations where the Sioux were given square or rectangular homes in which to live were demoralizing and humiliating for them due to their strong belief that the dwelling should be round or circular. There are probably numerous other examples of the circle in Dakota culture. Perhaps you can find other examples by reading resource books concerning the Dakota people.

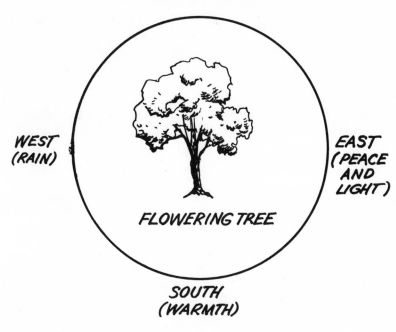

NORTH
(COLD AND WIND,
STRENGTH AND ENDURANCE)

WEST
(RAIN)

EAST
(PEACE
AND
LIGHT)

FLOWERING TREE

SOUTH
(WARMTH)

The Sacred Hoop of the Sioux Nation

The Significance of the Number 4
in Sioux Culture

The Sioux culture produced men of great philosophy who viewed experiences and sought explanations in terms of causes. They looked for and found in their culture those signs that indicated a unity of the universe as they knew it. Numbers played an important part in this philosophy and all powers were seen as emerging in a sort of hierarchy of 4's. Over all they believed was a unit of four powers, often considered as one whole power of the universe. Each of these four powers or parts was in turn made up of four powers, and so on down the line of their reasoning. It was on this foundation they built their explanation of the natural world, far too complex for men of other cultures to comprehend without extensive study.

Examples of this reverence to the numeral 4 can be found in the following references evident in the philosophy of Black Elk, in the book *Black Elk Speaks,* by Neihardt.

In speaking of a sacred pipe, Black Elk mentions the four ribbons which stood for the four quarters of the universe. The black ribbon represented the west, where thunder beings lived and sent the rain. The white ribbon stood for the north, whence the great white cleansing wind came. The east was represented by a red ribbon, and from this quarter light originated, and here the morning star lived, giving men wisdom. The yellow ribbon represented the south, whence comes the summer and the power to grow.

In his vision, Black Elk saw horses of four colors, black, white, sorrel, and buckskin. They appeared in formation four abreast and marched four by four.

Also in his vision, Black Elk was told by the spirits that he would walk upon the earth with his powers for four ascents or generations. (And he did.)

In speaking of a sacred herb, it was thought to grow and bear four blossoms, representing the four quarters of the earth.

In describing the Sun Dance, it was noted that those carrying the sacred tree to the dancing circle stopped four times, giving thanks at each stop to the four powers or seasons.

The Horse Dance, originated to interpret Black Elk's vision to his people, called for four black horses to represent the west, four white horses for the north, four sorrels to represent the east and four buckskins to represent the south. Four maidens or sacred virgins were designated to carry the symbols of power given to him by the spirits.

In sending forth a voice to the spirits, it seemed appropriate to repeat the words or phrases four times, and on one occasion it was noted that fasting was directed for four days.

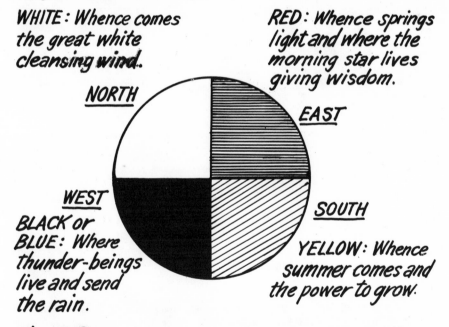

WHITE: Whence comes the great white cleansing wind.

NORTH

RED: Whence springs light and where the morning star lives giving wisdom.

EAST

WEST

BLACK or BLUE: Where thunder-beings live and send the rain.

SOUTH

YELLOW: Whence summer comes and the power to grow.

The 4 Powers or the One Whole Supreme Power of the Universe.

The Relationship of All Power

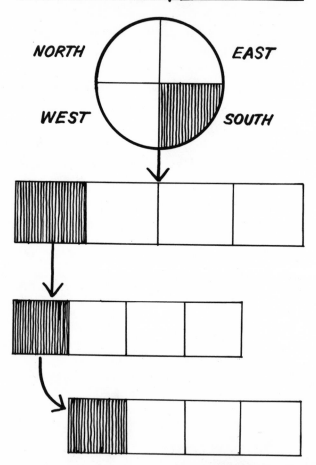

In this diagram South, one of the 4 great powers, produces 4 additional powers, and each of these 4 produces 4 more powers, creating a number base ranging from 1 to 4 to 16 to 64 or as far as necessary to carry the belief.

In describing the events of one of the tribal dances, it was said that the group marched and danced around the circle of the village four times.

Can you think of any instances in your own culture where the number four has significance? (How about the four-leaf clover?)

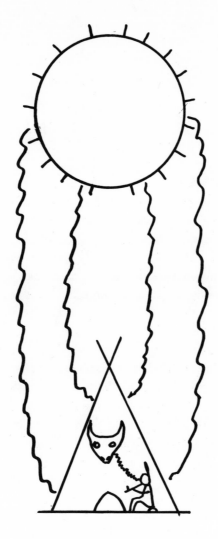

To the Sioux, the Everywhere Spirit operated through the sun. This action was usually depicted in Sioux art through the use of four wavy lines, relating to the four powers of the universe.

Note the sacred symbol of the buffalo on the tepee and the life-giving line connecting it to the figure of the man.

Religious Beliefs

The Sioux knew nothing of the Christian religion, of the Christian God, or of the biblical accounts of the creation, or of the Christian heaven, but they had developed their own deep religious beliefs long before the white missionaries came among them. Their great devotion to the things of nature and their desire to bring a logical explanation to their life created a religion that was both satisfying and rewarding. To this day, modern, traditional Sioux still practice their teachings, holy men are still found on the reservations, and the old ceremonies are still very much alive.

The white man's Christian belief that God sent His son to mankind, that He was crucified, and that He will return at the Last Judgment, or end of the world, is not so different from the Sioux teachings of hundreds of years ago, or in present day explanations of that belief.

The Indian knows that the Great Spirit sent someone to him in the form of an animal, who turned into human form and was called "White Buffalo Calf Maiden." She brought the sacred pipe to the Indian and foretold of seven visions that would be made known to the people. These visions would represent seven ways of praying to the Great Spirit. She also prophesied that she would appear again at the end of this world.

The Sioux were taught and understood that all things are of the Great Spirit. Trees, rivers, mountains, grass, four-legged animals, two-legged animals, and winged creatures all came from the Great Spirit called Wakantanka or Taku Wakan, and he is the Supreme Being.

Before the appearance of the Buffalo Calf Maiden, the Indian honored the Great Spirit but among the Sioux the coming of the Buffalo Calf Maiden brought a most important instrument, the peace pipe used in all ceremonies.

Calumet

The Sacred Pipe or Calumet

The Indian religion came into being many, many years ago. Two men of the Sans Arc tribe were hunting and saw something approaching in the distance. As it drew close they observed a beautiful maiden, dressed in white buckskin and carrying a bundle. One of the men had evil thoughts about this maiden and moved toward her. The other hunter tried to forcibly restrain him but the evil man pushed the good warrior away. A cloud descended on the evil one and when it lifted, his body was a skeleton having been devoured by worms. This symbolized that one who lives in ignorance and has evil in his heart may be destroyed by his own actions.

The maiden spoke to the remaining warrior, telling him not to be afraid but to return to his people and prepare them for her coming. This was done, and the beautiful maiden appeared in their midst walking among them in circular fashion in a sun-wise or clockwise direction. She took her bundle and giving it to the assembled chiefs said, "this is a

sacred gift and must always be treated in a holy way. In this bundle is a
sacred pipe which no impure man should ever see. With this sacred pipe
you will send your voices to Wakantanka, your Father and Grandfather.
With this sacred pipe you will walk upon the earth which is your Grandmother and Mother. All your steps should be holy. The bowl of the pipe
is red stone which represents the earth. A buffalo calf is carved in the
stone facing the center and symbolizes the four-legged creatures who live
as brothers among you. The stem is wood and represents all growing
things. Twelve feathers hang from where the stem fits the bowl and are
from the Spotted Eagle. These represent all the winged brothers who
live among you. All these things are joined to you who will smoke the
pipe and send voices to Wakantanka. When you use this pipe to pray,
you will pray for and with everything. The sacred pipe binds you to all
your relatives; your Grandfather and Father, your Grandmother and
Mother. The red stone represents the Mother Earth on which you will
live. The earth is red and the two-legged creatures who live upon it
are also red. Wakantanka has given you a red road (a good and straight
road) to travel and you must remember that all people who stand on
this earth are sacred. From this day the sacred pipe will stand on this red
earth and you will send your voices to Wakantanka. There are seven
circles on the stone which represent the seven rites in which you will
use the pipe."

The Buffalo Calf Maiden then instructed the chiefs to send runners
to the distant bands of the Sioux nation to bring in the many leaders.
This they did, and when the leaders assembled she instructed all of them
in the sacred ceremonies. She told them of the first rite, that of the keeping of the soul and told them that the remaining six rites would be made
known to them through visions. As she started to leave she said, "remember how sacred the pipe is and treat it in a sacred manner, for it will be
with you always. Remember also that in me are four ages. I will leave
you now but shall look upon you in every age and will return in the end."
The Sioux begged her to stay with them and promised that they would
aways care for her and provide for her, and would erect a lodge for her
but she said, "no, my Father above, the Great Spirit, is happy with you,
his grandchildren, and I must return to the spirit world."

She walked from their midst a short way, sat down and when she rose she had become a young, red and brown buffalo calf. She walked a little further, lay down and rolled, and rose as a white buffalo. She walked further, stopped and rose as a black buffalo. She then bowed to the four quarters of the universe and disappeared in the distance.

The seven rites or rituals of the sacred pipe, representing the seven ways of praying to Wakantanka are:

1. *The Keeping of the Soul.* This first ritual given to the Sioux by White Buffalo Calf Maiden was a rite in which the soul of a dead loved one is purified so that it might return to the Great Spirit, its point of origin. At a later time, perhaps a year later, another part of the ritual involves the releasing of the soul for its journey to the Great Spirit.

2. *Inipi: The Rite of Purification.* This sacred ritual of the sweat lodge is very holy and has been used through the years to make the people pure and to gain strength for some great undertaking. When one participates in these sacred rites he leaves behind in the sweat lodge all that is impure and emerges into the light purified in body and soul to live as the Great Spirit wishes. This rite brings the individual to a closer experience to the real world of the Great Spirit which is beyond this world. To those who have participated in the sacred rite it is as if they are born again and have done much to improve their own goodness and strength as well as the goodness and strength of the Sioux nation. The physical strength is tested in this ceremony, often as a group, and group participation bonds the participants closer together.

3. *Hanblecheyapi: Crying for a Vision.* This ritual is at the very center of the religion and everyone may attempt to receive great visions which will be interpreted by the holy men, giving strength and health to both the individual and to the people. Some material object related to the vision is carried by the individual so that the power will remain with him in this world. These objects are usually carried in sacred medicine bundles or worn on the body. The vision quest is a great preparatory ceremony for young people about to depart into the challenge of the adult world. It provides a complete time in which they may seriously reflect upon where they will embark occupationally and spiritually. The Inipi (sweat bath) is usually a preparatory ceremony for a young Sioux about to do the vision quest.

4. *Wiwanyag Wachipi: The Sun Dance.* This sacred ritual was divided into two periods of four days each and was an annual coming together of all the people. The first period was used in preparing for the Sun Dance and assembling each tepee into its traditional location within the camp circle. Friends and relatives were united and family bonds renewed and strengthened. Tribal spirit and unity were revitalized and relationship to the Great Spirit was purified and made new again. The second period was devoted to participation by all in the sacred rituals of the dance. The vision quest was an individual ceremony for inner peace and strength, whereas the Sun Dance exists for tribal unity, peace, and strength, through the honoring and thanksgiving offered to the Great Spirit. The Sioux do not worship the sun per se, but acknowledge that the sun was placed in the universe by the Great Spirit so that "the people might live."

5. *Hunkapi: The Making of Relatives.* These sacred rites are based on three ideals of peace in the following order of importance:

1. Peace comes to the souls of men when they realize or recognize their relationship to the universe and to the Great Spirit, who is at the center of the universe. This center is everywhere, even in the souls of men.
2. Peace between two individuals, recognizing the overall brotherhood of man in relation to the universe.
3. Peace that is made between two nations, recognizing that all men of all nations are as brothers, and as children of the Great Spirit. This sacred rite establishes a relationship on earth which reflects the spiritual relationship between man and the Great Spirit.

6. *Ishna Ta Awi Cha Lowan: Preparing a Girl for Womanhood.* This sacred ritual recognizes the importance of the woman as the source of the flowering tree of the Sioux nation. It teaches the young girl that she will be as Mother Earth and will bear children who shall be brought up in a holy manner. The ceremonial rites are a source of much holiness for the woman and for the entire Sioux nation.

The older a woman becomes in the Sioux nation the more powerful she is regarded, since her acquired wisdom is always listened to and respected by all. It is the woman who sits at the place of honor holding the sacred pipe in the spirit ceremony because after all, it was a woman, "White Buffalo Calf Maiden," who brought the sacred pipe and the seven ceremonies to the people. It is a virgin girl that will take the first cut on the Sun Dance tree so that it may be later felled and brought to the center of the arena.

7. *Tapa Wanka Yap: The Throwing of the Ball.* This sacred ritual which developed over the years into a game was originally a ritual in which all participants were able to have the ball. The ball used in this ceremony was symbolic of Wakantanka and the universe. In the ceremony a small girl stands at the center of the circle of participants and throws the ball from the center of the circle outward to the four quarters of the universe. This symbolizes that Wakantanka is everywhere and as the ball descends upon the participants so likewise does the power of the Great Spirit. The small child is at the center representing eternal youth and purity as befitting one who came recently from Wakantanka to the people. This ritual established the relationship of the people to the universe or Great Spirit that is everywhere.

The sacred pipe, given to the Sioux by White Buffalo Calf Maiden is used in all the foregoing rites as a sacred object around which all the ceremonies are centered.

The Buffalo Calf Maiden also told the Sioux where to find the sacred red stone from which to make the sacred pipes. This is located at the pipestone quarries in southwestern Minnesota, near the town of Pipestone. It was here that the Sioux were to dig for their pipestone and all other Indian nations were to be allowed to dig there also in peace and to be allowed free access to the site by the dominant tribe in the area. The Sioux allowed all nations to enter the quarry peacefully and this is perhaps the first evidence of a true United Nations organization in action.

The Sioux believed in many spirits or powers beneath the all-powerful Great Spirit. Most of these powers were believed to be associated with the winds, the thunder, and other natural parts of the environment.

One of the greatest of their powers was "Wahkeenyan" the Thunder Being who lived in a lodge on top of a high mountain. At his East door was a butterfly; at the West a bear; at the South a fawn; and at the North a reindeer. He made axes and spears and was so large that when he walked on the earth he left great "thunder tracks" (large depressions that one might see in rock formations, such as those near Big Stone Lake in western Minnesota).

Another spirit power was "Hayokah" or "Heyoka," the being of opposites who viewed all things backward. He called hard things soft, smooth things rough, white things black, and was said to smile with pain and to groan with joy. Dances were often held in his honor in order to cheer up the people during troubled times or to reverse a situation when things were not going well for the tribe. Heyoka at times takes the form of people and mingles with them doing things contrary. Some people are even possessed to a small degree with "Heyoka," doing things the opposite of which is expected of them, and when least expected.

The Sioux also believed in a sacred buffalo spirit or power who looked after the buffalo. The Sioux were very careful not to displease this spirit by killing too many buffalo and therefore killed only what their food supply demanded. It was believed that the Great Spirit especially cared for Tatanka the Buffalo, therefore this spirit was provided by Him.

We can say of the Sioux, that they were deeply religious people, and that they lived faithfully by their beliefs, and that their belief was a strong, unifying force that bound them together in a highly organized way of life. Through their religion they found personal peace and satisfaction as well as an explanation for the mysteries of life.

The artist George Catlin, who lived for eight years among 48 North American Plains Indian tribes, said: "All history of the subject goes to prove that when first visited by civilized people, the American Indians have been found friendly and hospitable—from the days of Christopher Columbus to the Lewis and Clark Expedition . . . and so also have a great many other travelers, including myself. Nowhere, to my knowledge, have they stolen a six-pence worth of my property, though in their countries there are no laws to punish for theft. I have visited forty-eight different tribes, and I feel authorized to say that the North American Indian in his native state is honest, hospitable, faithful, brave . . . and an honorable and religious being . . ."

George Catlin's Creed About American Indians

I love a people who have always made me welcome to the best they had.

I love a people who are honest without laws, who have no jails and no poorhouses.

I love a people who keep the commandments without ever having read them or heard them preached from the pulpit.

I love a people who never swear, who never take the name of God in vain.

I love a people "who love their neighbors as they love themselves!"

I love a people who worship God without a Bible, for I believe that God loves them also.

I love a people whose religion is all the same, and who are free from religious animosities.

I love a people who have never raised a hand against me, or stolen my property, where there was no law to punish for either.

I love a people who have never fought a battle with white men, except on their own ground.

I love and don't fear mankind where God has made and left them, for there they are children.

I love a people who live and keep what is their own without locks and keys.

I love all people who do the best they can. And oh, how I love a people who don't live for the love of money!

The Sun Dance

The Sun Dance was a very important cultural observance to the Sioux. It was many things, a time of festive reunion, renewing the relationship to nature, and the preparation for life and death. In some ways it would compare to the white culture observance of Mother's Day, Father's Day, May Day, and all religious observances all grouped into one grand observance. This was usually an annual affair, held in June, or the Moon of Making Fat. This month represented the time at which the sun was at its highest point and when nature's plants were entering a season of growth, following the winter of dormant existence. It was intended to purify the body and soul of the individual and to call upon the unseen powers for blessings and power.

To the white culture this observance seemed uncivilized and people looked at only the physical torture inflicted on male members of the dance in drawing their conclusions. This painful portion of the Sun Dance was not required of anyone, and only those wishing to show their bravery or to gain special powers from the spirits elected to participate.

The Dakota viewed this sacrificial offering of pain as a means of seeking power to escape death or to gain supernatural power over enemies, and since the price to pay was high, only a few strong-willed individuals participated in the ritual. Those who did participate were viewed with much admiration by their people. It has been reported that the famous medicine man of the Teton Sioux, Sitting Bull, had many scars on his chest and back to remind one that he had participated often in this quest for power.

The usual ritual called for a cut to be made on the chest or back, through which a strip of rawhide was threaded and then tied to the tree

A Tribal Dance Participant

at the center of the dance circle. The participant would then dance and sing and cry out to the spirits for pity and the granting of power. If the person fainted from pain, this was considered good since he then was in a state of communion with the spirits.

The U. S. Government, after placing the Sioux on reservations, prohibited them from including this practice in their dances.

The following quotation by Black Elk, in *Black Elk Speaks,* by Neihardt, describes the Sun Dance held just prior to the historic Little Bighorn Battle, and many of the Dakota people, especially the ardent followers of Sitting Bull, were convinced that the power gained through this dance enabled them to crush Custer's forces in that battle.

In the white man's culture, one wore medals and ribbons as badges of honors gained, or one might have occasion to describe various college degrees as symbols of achievement. To the Sioux, the scars of the Sun Dance were equally symbolic of achievement.

※

THE SUN DANCE

(As described by Black Elk*)

"About the middle of the Moon of Making Fat (June), the whole village moved a little way up the river to a good place for a sun dance. The valley was wide and flat there, and we camped in a great oval with the water flowing through it, and in the center they built the bower of branches in a circle for the dancers, with the opening of it to the east (from whence the light comes). Scouts were sent out in all directions to guard the sacred place. Sitting Bull, who was the greatest medicine man of the nation at that time, had charge of this dance to purify the people and to give them power and endurance. It was held in the Moon of Fatness because that is the time when the sun is highest and the growing power of the world is strongest.

". . . First a holy man was sent out to find the 'waga chun' (cottonwood tree), the holy tree that should stand in the middle of the dancing circle. Nobody dared to follow to see what he did or hear the sacred words he would say there. And when he had found the right tree, he would tell the people, and they would come there singing, with flowers all over them. Then when they had gathered around the holy tree, some women who were bearing children would dance around it, because the Spirit of the Sun loves all fruitfulness. After that, a warrior who had done some brave deed that summer struck the tree, counting coup on it, and when he had done this, he had to give gifts to those who had least of everything, and the braver he was, the more he gave away.

*From *Black Elk Speaks*, by Neihardt, University of Nebraska Press, pages 95-98, 1961. University of Nebraska Press.

"After this, a band of young maidens came singing, with sharp axes in their hands; and they had to be so good that nobody there could say anything against them, or that any man had ever known them; and it was the duty of anyone who knew anything bad about any of them to tell it right before all the people there and prove it. But if anybody lied, it was very bad for him.

"The maidens chopped the tree down and trimmed its branches off. Then chiefs who were the sons of chiefs carried the sacred tree home, stopping four times on the way, once for each season, giving thanks for each.

"Now when the tree had been brought home but was not yet set up in the center of the dancing place, mounted warriors gathered around the circle of the village, and at a signal they all charged inward upon the center where the tree would stand, each trying to be the first to touch the sacred place; and whoever was the first could not be killed in war that year. When they all came together in the middle, it was like a battle, with the ponies rearing and screaming in a big dust and the men shouting and wrestling and trying to throw each other off the horses.

"After that there was a big feast and plenty for everybody to eat, and a big dance just as though we had won a victory.

"The next day the tree was planted in the center by holy men who sang sacred songs and made sacred vows to the spirit. And the next morning nursing mothers brought their holy little ones to lay them at the bottom of the tree, so that the sons would be brave men and the daughters the mothers of brave men. The holy men pierced the ears of the little ones, and for each piercing the parents gave away a pony to someone who was in need.

"The next day the dancing began, and those who were going to take part were ready, for they had been fasting and purifying themselves in the sweat lodges, and praying. First, their bodies were painted by the holy men. Then each would lie down beneath the tree as though he were dead, and the holy men would cut a place in his back or chest, so that a strip of rawhide, fastened to the top of the tree, could be pushed through the flesh

and tied. Then the man would get up and dance to the drums, leaning on
the rawhide strip as long as he could stand the pain or until the flesh
tore loose."

THE GHOST DANCE

(The following background of the Ghost Dance is based upon infor-
mation to be found in the book *Indians of the United States,* by Wissler.)

The Plains Indians, by 1885, were faced with a serious crisis. The
buffalo had disappeared and this meant not only a loss of their major food
supply, but materials for both clothing and shelter. A tepee covered with
buffalo skins was warm in winter, and buffalo robes were a warm item
of clothing. These were no longer available. Cloth-covered tepees were
cold, and the wool blankets available in the white man's market were
too expensive to buy. These losses led to a severe economic collapse, a
depression such as had never been known before to these people. The
Government saw to it that the Sioux did not starve, as they provided
rations of crackers, salt pork, flour and beef. These foods did not take the
place of good fresh buffalo meat however, and often the beef rations were
slow in arriving. Suffering was widespread among the Sioux in winter
months, as they were subjected to freezing weather and epidemics of
"white man's diseases" such as whooping cough and measles. Young children died in great numbers due to these conditions.

Sioux leaders became discouraged and resentful at the state of conditions. The buffalo was gone, they were no longer permitted to go on
horse-raiding parties and time was passed by waiting for the Government
to deliver the necessities of life.

A people who had depended upon nature for their existence seemed
now at the mercy of nature as they were encouraged to farm, often on land
unsuitable for farming. In the Sioux nature-culture, farming had no place.
It was degrading for them to do this, and considered the work of the
women. They longed for the days gone by, when they were free to roam
the plains and to hunt the once-plentiful buffalo.

They lived in past memories and in hope that the future would hold
promise for them. This hope, although badly shattered, was rekindled

almost overnight. Far to the west, in Nevada, there was rumored to be a sacred man among the Paiutes, who had talked to a Great Spirit, in a vision, and was told how to save the Indian people. He was told also that the wasichus (white people) could be made to disappear, and that the buffalo could be brought back. Relatives, long dead, could be brought back and there would be a new earth. This man was called the wanekia (one who makes life), and was the son of the Great Spirit. His Indian name was Wovoka.

He said there was another world coming, just like a cloud. It would come out of the west like a whirlwind, and would crush everything on this earth which was old and dying. In this new world, meat would be plentiful, as in the old days, and all dead relatives would be alive again, and all the buffalo which had ever been killed would be alive and roaming the plains.

Many of the Sioux believed this to be their salvation, and those who didn't believe, wanted to so earnestly that a delegation of chiefs was sent to far-off Nevada to talk with this holy man. It is not known whether this wanekia actually did talk to the Sioux delegation, or whether in their desperate quest for hope they added the fuel of their imaginations to the fire. At any rate they returned to the plains with great stories and a missionary zeal that fired their people to new heights of endeavor.

It was said that the wanekia had given some sacred red paint and two sacred eagle feathers to the visitors, telling them to return to their people and to put the paint on their faces. They were to dance a ghost dance, which he taught to them. If they would do this, they might get in the other world when it came and the wasichus would not be able to get on and would disappear. The eagle feathers would cause lost relatives to come back to life in the new world. It was said that the wanekia had first come to the white people a long time ago and that they had killed him, so he was coming to the Indians this time. All this was to take place after one more winter, when the grass appeared in the spring (1891).

A ghost dance was held by the Sioux north of Pine Ridge, and people who danced saw their dead relatives and talked with them. A dance was also held at Wounded Knee, and soon the ghost dance was evident all over the Sioux reservations.

The dancing continued and the white population and Indian agents became alarmed. It appeared to them as if the Sioux were preparing an uprising. This rumor spread rapidly and soon a large buildup of soldiers was noted at Pine Ridge and surrounding posts, in anticipation of trouble. The Indian agent made a ruling that the Sioux could dance only three days each month and that the rest of the time should be spent in working for a living. Plans were made to arrest those leaders who seemed to be leading the ghost dance movement. This created a situation in which many Sioux ran away from the reservations to escape punishment, and this convinced the Government that an uprising was underway. In an attempt to arrest Sitting Bull on his reservation he resisted and was killed. This act caused many Sioux to begin thinking of fighting back, and several bands ran away from the reservations.

One band of nearly four hundred, led by Big Foot, had spent part of the winter in the Badlands. They suffered such hardships that they finally chose to return to the reservation in order to survive. Detachments of soldiers were roaming the plains looking for them when they finally made contact. The little band surrendered peacefully and made camp at Wounded Knee, surrounded by soldiers and cannon. The next day an incident provoked by the officers in charge, while confiscating weapons, resulted in the bloody massacre of the entire band, including women, children and small babies.

This action spawned several small-scale battles in which the Sioux were the hunted and the Army the hunter. Chief Red Cloud, who had given up fighting long ago, advised all the bands to think of their women and children and to return to the reservations. This they did, and the remnants of many suffering bands straggled back to the reservation, under military custody.

It was over. The dreams were ended. The hope rekindled in the hearts and souls of the Sioux by the Ghost Dance had been shattered. Did all hope die with the massacre at Wounded Knee or does it still exist in the hearts and minds of later generations of this proud race?

TREATIES WITH THE INDIANS

Lt. Pike Speaking to the Sioux

Pike's Treaty of 1805

Lieutenant Zebulon Pike, dashing military leader, scout, hunter, surveyor, geologist, astronomer and man of many callings, was sent by the U. S. Government to the Minnesota Territory in 1805, to expel British traders from the area. They were to have moved out following the Revolutionary War, but the rich fur trade with the Indians was so profitable they neglected to move.

Lieutenant Pike went to Kaposia, the small Sioux village south of St. Paul, and made friends with the tribe. He made his main camp on the big island at the mouth of the Minnesota River, just below where Fort Snelling was later located. This island was named Pike Island in his honor.

Pike summoned the Sioux chiefs to discuss a treaty proposal. He obtained for the U. S. Government a piece of land nine miles on each side of the river. The Sioux were to retain hunting and fishing rights, and the payment for this land consisted of about two thousand dollars worth of various types of merchandise. (Probably items new and appealing to the Sioux people.)

The Sioux thought they had made a fair bargain. After all, what was such a small land concession compared to the enormous expanse of territory they called theirs? Little did they know this was to be the first of many such treaty dealings that would eventually relieve them of all their domain.

Lieutenant Pike was an eloquent speaker, even through translation, and the following speech is said to have won the trust of the Sioux people.

". . . Brothers, I am happy to meet with you at this council fire, which your father has sent me to kindle, and to take you by the hands as our children. We have but lately acquired from the Spanish the extensive

76

territory of Louisiana. Our general has thought proper to sent out a number of his warriors to visit all his red children, and to tell them his will and to hear what request they may have to make of their father. I am happy the choice has fallen on me to come this road as I find my brothers, the Sioux, ready to listen to my words. . . . Brothers, these posts are intended as a benefit to you. It is the intention of the United States to establish at these posts, factories in which the Indians may procure all their things at a cheaper and better rate than they do now or than your traders can afford to sell them to you. Brothers, I expect that you will give orders to all your young warriors to respect my flag, and protection which I may extend to the Chippewa chiefs who may come down with me in the spring; for as a dog runs to my lodge for safety, his enemy must walk over me to hurt him."

Fond du Lac Treaty of 1826

The Sioux and Chippewa had much trouble about the land where both wanted to fish and hunt. The U. S. Government decided to help both tribes by making dividing lines between their hunting grounds. A meeting or council was held at Fond du Lac, near Duluth, and notes of history describe this meeting as a major production.

The government agents brought with them a band, and the stirring notes of "Hail Columbia" were rendered periodically as a sort of council theme song. The agents' boat or barge was gaily decorated with flags and red, white, and blue streamers, truly indicative of the importance of the "great white father."

There were seven tribes represented and there was much speechmaking and feasting. This continued for five days, and in an effort to speed up negotiations, the agents suggested that the many gifts they had brought would not be given out until the council was over. This technique worked so well that it appears to have been adopted as a standard procedure for conducting treaties thereafter.

The Chippewas promised not to wage war against the Sioux and to hunt only in certain areas. They promised to give up their allegiance to the British, and to surrender four of their number to the Government, for their part in the killing of four white people at Lake Pepin earlier.

This treaty did much to hold down trouble between the two nations, at least for a short time, but more important, it established the U. S. Government as the power with whom both tribes should be concerned from that time on.

Fort Snelling Treaty of 1837

A council was held at Fort Snelling in 1837 involving the U. S. Government and the Chippewas. After the usual council proceedings and merrymaking, the results of the treaty gave the U. S. all the pine forests on the St. Croix River and all rivers that flowed into it. This immense tract of land and unknown wealth was bought for less than two cents an acre. It represented the first major attempt to obtain land from the Chippewa for the white man's benefit.

Sioux Land Session of 1837

The same year the Chippewa were giving up vast expanses of northeast Minnesota, the Sioux were invited to send representatives to Washington to discuss the status of their land east of the Mississippi. Many white people were eager and waiting to settle this area, but were fearful of what the Sioux reaction might be. This meeting must have been very impressive to the Sioux leaders for they were pursuaded to give up all their land east of the Mississippi. Within twenty-four hours, most of this land was staked out in claims by white settlers.

Fort Snelling Council of 1850

The Sioux and Chippewa, all councils and treaties to the contrary, remained bitter enemies and many battles and raids were originated by both nations.

Governor Ramsey, in 1850, called representatives of both tribes to a council at Fort Snelling. He wanted to settle their quarrels and chose the fort as the meeting site so that he might have access to both soldiers and cannon if the need presented.

Results of the council were doomed from the start. The Sioux, in an effort to polish their image as a great power to be highly regarded, planned a late arrival. Some people felt that this was an effort to throw fear into the hearts of the Chippewa. Their arrival, carefully staged, saw the tall (6 feet 6 inches) Chief Sitting in a Row lead the Sioux over the crest of a hill in a mock charge at the council site. Arriving amid much yelling and firing of weapons into the air, they must have indeed been something to behold.

The council got underway, and at one point the Sioux chiefs got up and walked away in their resentment over having white women in attendance. They said they had come to talk with chiefs, not with women. The Chippewa capitalized on this opportunity as Chief Hole in the Day politely asked the white ladies to sit on the Chippewa side of the line.

Both tribes were scolded and threatened by Governor Ramsey, and cautioned not to make trouble in the future. The council ended, and it is possible that all parties went away feeling a sense of victory, although nothing was really resolved.

Traverse Des Sioux Treaty of 1851

Pioneers in early Minnesota wanted the Sioux land west of the Mississippi River. They wanted it for farms and for the timber. They wanted cheap land and the Sioux stood between them and their goal. Much pressure was brought to bear on the government, until Governor Ramsey and Luke Lea were appointed by the Commissioners of Indian Affairs to act as agents in buying this land from the Sioux. They made two treaties, one with the Upper Sioux tribes at Traverse Des Sioux, and another with the Lower Sioux tribes at Mendota. The Traverse Des Sioux treaty is described here.

Ramsey and Lea arrived at Traverse Des Sioux on June 30, 1851. Sioux chiefs at this meeting were: Red Iron, Sleepy Eye, Having the Face of a Star, Running Walker, and Curly Head. The Sioux, as was their custom, brought many of their people with them. The encampment took on the appearance of a giant campground, and the people enjoyed games, races and tribal dancing. Some food was provided by the Government. Discussion and debate over the sale of the land dragged on for several days, and most of the food was held back until such time as an agreement could be reached. There are some who feel that this delaying tactic was used as a sort of bait or reward to get the chiefs to sign the treaty.

The chiefs present were finally enticed to sign the treaty, and by doing so gave up all their land in Iowa and Minnesota east of a line drawn from the Red River, Lake Traverse and the Big Sioux. They retained possession of a strip of land extending ten miles on either side of the Minnesota River, from Lake Traverse to the Yellow Medicine River. This narrow remnant of land was to be preserved for their home. For the sale of their land the Sioux were promised payment of $1,665,000. Only $305,000 was to be paid at once, and the balance was to be paid to them in yearly payments of $68,000. There were strings attached to this agreement, however, for part of this money was to be paid back to the Government for building schools, farms and mills and for other things such as equipment to be used on the farms.

The chiefs were influenced to sign this agreement, and at the same time were tricked into signing another agreement which gave most of their money to the fur traders present at the meeting. The traders said that they had sold goods to the tribes on credit, in trade for furs which were to be brought in at the close of the season. They said many of these debts had not been paid, and claimed the Sioux money. The Government agents supported this claim to the treaty money, and the Sioux went from the meeting unaware of what had taken place.

The end results of this treaty were:

1. The Sioux gave up nearly all their land in Minnesota.

2. Their payment money was claimed by the traders for real or imaginary debts.

3. They were deceived into signing the traders' debt papers without knowing what they were signing.

4. The yearly payments of $68,000 were later to become another deception, as payments were slow in coming, if they came at all, in succeeding years. This caused hardship and mistrust of the white government and was a major cause of the war that was to break out in 1862.

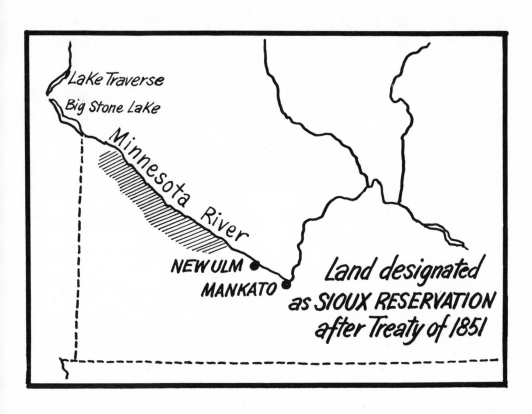

Mendota Treaty of 1851

Ramsey and Lea, returning from their successful treaty encounter at Traverse Des Sioux with the Upper Sioux tribes, wasted no time in pressing for similar agreement with the chiefs of the Lower Sioux tribes. They met with these chiefs, one of whom was Little Crow, at Mendota two weeks later, and used much the same procedure that had worked for them earlier. Again large stocks of food were kept in reserve for feasting after the signing of the treaty.

The fur traders were in attendance again, and again the chiefs signed agreements with the traders, authorizing the Government to deduct debt payments from the land-sale money. The same sort of cash and annuity payments were given to the Lower Sioux as had been given to the Upper Sioux tribes. When the chiefs signed, they were paid $30,000, which had been promised them from a previous treaty in 1837. This money had been held back for fear that if the Sioux had all that money, they would not sign future treaties. History tells us that most of this $30,000 was spent in St. Paul over the next few days as the Sioux went on a gigantic shopping spree. Thus the white settlers not only got the land from the Sioux, but the money came back, too, in a strange turn of economic events.

The two treaties, both negotiated within a two-week period, managed to obtain for the white settlers all the land that had been used for hunting and living by the Sioux for hundreds of years.

Fort Laramie Treaty of 1868

The Western Sioux, after several years of fighting, in which they attempted to drive out the soldiers and settlers in their hunting land, grew weary of war and sat down to talk a treaty with the white government.

The terms of the treaty, insisted on and gained by Chief Red Cloud for his people, contained the following points:

1. All forts in the Sioux land of northern Wyoming and lower Montana were to be removed, leaving only one major fort, that at Fort Laramie.

2. The Black Hills region (Paha sapa), long a sacred area of the Sioux, was to be retained by them as a place to hunt, fish and live forever.

Peace came to the area for a few years, but this treaty, like all others, was soon to be broken.

In 1874, Lieut. Col. George Custer was sent out on an expedition from Fort Lincoln, in North Dakota, to explore the Black Hills for the U. S. Government. On this expedition, gold was discovered, and this news was flashed around the nation. Immediately, scores of gold seekers invaded the land. The Government tried to uphold the treaty for a time, and established several posts from which they proceeded to escort all gold seekers to the edge of the treaty land. This did not succeed, since the gold-hungry prospectors would turn around and go right back into the area.

The Government then tried another tactic. They offered to buy the Black Hills from the Sioux. The Sioux did not want to sell this sacred land at any price, and Chief Red Cloud, acting for the Sioux, placed such a high price on the land that it was impossible to consider. The Government offered six million dollars for the land, but Red Cloud said that it would take a hundred times that amount. Indian attacks soon became so frequent that the Government decided to protect the lives of its citizens, even though they were trespassing on treaty grounds.

The decision was reached that the Sioux must go. In December of 1875, the Secretary of Indian Affairs and the Secretary of the Interior issued an ultimatum that all Sioux not back on their established Missouri River reservations by January 31, 1876, would be considered hostile and dealt with by military force. This message was dispersed to the bands of Sioux throughout the Wyoming-Montana plains area by runners. Severe winter conditions made this impossible for the Sioux to obey (even if they had wanted to), and so the January 31 deadline passed and the Sioux had not returned.

It is interesting to note that even the runners who had delivered the messages did not make it back by the deadline due to the severity of the winter on the plains. It is difficult to imagine just how the Government agents expected large bands of Sioux families to travel hundreds of miles in freezing winter weather. Perhaps they didn't care, or maybe they had already made up their minds that war was the only answer. The Secretary of the Interior then washed his hands of the entire matter and turned it over to the Secretary of War. Plans were rapidly made to conduct a major campaign against the disobedient Sioux.

War had come again to the Sioux nation, and again it had been originated by the dishonoring of a treaty by the white government.

Little Crow's Dilemma

A band of four Sioux warriors, hungry and resentful at the actions of the white man's government toward them, lit the fuse to an explosive frontier war in August 1862.

Most accounts of this incident indicate that the four Sioux warriors stole eggs from a farm near Acton, in Meeker County, Minnesota. Fearful of being discovered or found out, they challenged the settlers to a sharp-shooting contest, turned their guns on the settlers, killing three men and two women. Word of this act traveled rapidly through the tribes of the Minnesota River Valley, and a council was called to determine what to do.

The council fire burned brightly and there was excitement in the air. The young warriors wanted to go to war, while some of the elders of the tribe were against such an action. Little Crow, one of the most highly respected chiefs at the council, listened silently as the warriors demanded war. He finally spoke, cautioning against war by making the following speech. (This is the author's judgment of what was probably said, arrived at by reading the various accounts of what was or might have been said.)

"... I have been to the Great City in the East and have seen the Great White Father. At that time I saw his cities, his soldiers and his guns. We are few in number compared to them. We might win some victories, but they will send soldiers from the east, with guns and cannon to fight us. Still I am your chief, and I must do what I think is best for our tribe. I know that we have been treated badly. The white man's ways are not our ways. I understand that your hunger is forcing you to act badly.

"You found some eggs that belonged to a white settler . . . you killed three white men and two women. We call this an act of war. We think it is right and honorable to kill our enemies and to take food for our women and children. The white man does not call this war. He calls it murder. They will demand that our warriors be delivered to them. They will kill them in a dishonorable way. They will hang them. You tell me now is the time to attack. The Great White Father's soldiers are fighting each other in the South (Civil War). They are too weak to help the white settlers who have taken our land. This may be so. Still my heart is heavy.

"I am a Dakota, your chief. Our wise men advise me to deliver our warriors to the white soldiers. Then we will not be bothered and keep peace. . . . But I know the white man will not stop. He will demand more land, and in the end we will not be free. We will no longer be able to roam the forests. We will have to work like women in fields raising corn and squash, pigs and cows. If you decide to make war . . . I shall lead you as my forefathers have done. It may be better to die like a man and enter the Hunting Grounds in the Great Beyond, where no white man can steal our game, than to die slowly without honor.

"As your chief, I must think of what is best for all of you. I warn you that the white man is stronger than you think . . . you may be defeated."

Many warriors, eager to get the war underway, taunted Little Crow, saying that he was a coward and had lived with the white men too long. The following account of Little Crow's reply is quoted as accurately as the author has determined it from various records.

Little Crow Speaks of Peace and War

Little Crow's Speech

"You call Little Crow a coward. Little Crow is not a coward and he is not a fool. When did he run away from his enemies? When did he leave his braves in battle and turn back to his tepee? When you retreated from your enemies, he walked behind you, facing the enemy, covering your backs like a bear covers her cubs. Is Little Crow without scalps? Look at his war feathers, behold the scalp locks of his enemies hanging from his lodgepole. Do they call him a coward? Little Crow is not a coward and he is not a fool.

"Braves, you are like little children. You know not what you are doing. You are full of the white man's devil-water, whisky. You are like dogs in the hot moon when they go mad and snap at their own shadows. We are only little herds of buffalo left scattered. The great herds that once covered the prairies are no more. The white men are like locusts when they fly so thick the whole sky is a snowstorm. You may kill one, two, ten, yes, as many as the leaves on the forest yonder, and their brothers will not miss them. Kill one or two and ten times ten will come to kill you. Count your fingers all day long and the white men with guns in their hands will come faster than you can count.

"Yes, they fight among themselves way off. Do you hear the thunder of their big guns? It would take you two moons to run down to where they are fighting and all the way your path would be among white soldiers as thick as the tamaracks among the swamps of the Chippewa. Yes, they fight among themselves, but you strike one of them and they will all turn on you and devour you and your women and your little children just as the locusts fall on the trees and devour all of the leaves in one day. You are fools and you will die like rabbits when the hungry wolves hunt them in the hard moon of January. Little Crow is no coward . . . he will die with you."

Following this speech, there was much celebrating on the part of the young warriors. Little Crow put on the war paint and with a heavy heart prepared to lead his people into war.

The Hanging of 38 Sioux

The Sioux Uprising or war of 1862 was a bloody page in the history of Minnesota and the nation. The Sioux or Dakota tribes had gone through the bleak winter of 1861 with scarcely enough food to survive. When spring came, they went to the Government agency to get their promised amount of food and clothing as well as money due on their annual agreement with the Government for sale of their lands. They found that the food and clothing were locked up in the storehouse, but their money had not yet been received from Washington. The agent refused to distribute the food and clothing until the money arrived, and to make matters worse, the traders would not extend any credit to the tribes.

The disappointment and plight of the Sioux turned to feelings of anger and resentment. Feelings ran high among the tribes, and it was decided to go to war with the white government. They felt strongly that the white government had robbed them of their land, their freedom and their right to expect fair treatment under the terms of their treaties. They resented, too, the attempt to force a new language and a new religion on them. They saw their existence threatened by the white man's failure to recognize their problems. Some chiefs advised against war, but in the end their warnings went unheeded. The first attacks of the war were directed against settlers and traders with later attacks coming against towns and forts.

To the Sioux, war meant fighting, killing, and what white people called "massacre." This was their cultural way of dealing with an enemy. To the white population of Minnesota, these acts were considered those of "savages" and they were determined that these savages were to be punished to the fullest extent possible.

THE
SIOUX UPRISING

Major Battle Sites

ACTON
LOWER AGENCY
REDWOOD FERRY
BIRCH COULEE
UPPER
AGENCY
FORT RIDGELY
WOOD LAKE
NEW ULM

Minnesota River

Mississippi R.

This frontier war cost many lives and property losses, and delayed the settlement of the state for a short time. The Sioux were unable to cope with the Government troops and weapons, and went down to defeat.

Some three hundred and seven captured Sioux were condemned to death for their part in the war. Henry B. Whipple, bishop of the Episcopal Church in Minnesota, intervened in the Indians' behalf and went directly to Washington, where he presented their case to President Lincoln. Lincoln decided that most of these Indians had been fighting in a war just as white soldiers fight in a war. These he determined should not be punished. There were some he felt were guilty of murder or other serious crimes and these he ordered to be hanged.

On December 26, 1862, thirty-eight Sioux men were hanged at a public mass execution at Mankato, and with their passing the Sioux nation virtually disappeared from the state. The white population insisted that the Sioux be moved out of Minnesota, and public opinion was so strong that the Government ended all treaties with the Sioux, stopped their annuity payments, took their Minnesota River lands from them and moved them west to the Missouri River country. The Sioux had made a desperate attempt to hold what they believed to be rightfully theirs, but failed. The final tragedy saw thirty-eight of their people put to death in a sort of carnival atmosphere which some historians have labeled "America's greatest mass execution." It may have been the largest, but one has to question the word "greatest."

In the spring of 1863, all remaining Sioux in Minnesota, except for a small number of trusted individuals, were removed from the state and placed on a reservation in Nebraska.

For three years after the end of this conflict, military expeditions ranged over the prairies in search of "outlawed" Indians, and thus the uprising continued for several more years.

Other Sioux tribes rose against the white man in the next few years and it was not until the battle or "massacre" at Wounded Knee in 1890 that the Indian war was over.

The spirit of rebellion, the Sioux vow to fight for what they thought was theirs, was kindled into flame in Minnesota, and the resulting fire spread rapidly over the Upper Midwest, burning through such historic encounters as the Rosebud, the Little Bighorn, and finally the "massacre" at Wounded Knee.

The blaze was extinguished by the expanding white government, and the Dakota nation was broken and scattered to the winds of history.

U. S. Army Campaigns Against the Sioux

The tide of white settlers had advanced westward to the Mississippi River by 1832. The Wisconsin Territory, organized in 1836, had a population of over 12,000, and by 1837 the Sioux in Minnesota began giving up their land to the intruding white government.

The white tide flowed across the Mississippi, and the Minnesota Territory was organized in 1849. Population in this area reached 157,000 by 1857, and the following year statehood was established. The desire for the Sioux land was so strong that the Sioux were forced to give more and more land to the white government. This land acquisition, along with the failure of the white government to honor its treaty agreements, led to the Sioux war of 1862. (See Little Crow's Dilemma.)

The Western Sioux, at about this same time, also began to rise up and fight for their rights. The discovery of gold in the West brought thousands of white treasure-seekers into the Sioux land. The Oregon and California trails were routed directly through Sioux hunting land. Buffalo were slaughtered and dispersed by the emigrants, and the Sioux fought back by attacking wagon trains. The Government sought to resolve this situation, and in a great council held at Fort Laramie in 1851, had its agents meet with over ten thousand Sioux. Results of this council were that tribal boundaries were set up, and for the right to travel safely through Sioux country, the Government agreed to pay $50,000 each year. It was further stated that should the Sioux violate the treaty terms, the payments would be stopped.

Both parties to the treaty promptly ignored it, and trouble continued until 1854, when an incident triggered an all-out war on the plains. A

Mormon group traveling through the Sioux country had a cow wander from its procession into a Sioux village. A warrior killed the cow for food, and immediately the air was tense with hostility. A young Army officer, with a twenty-nine man troop, marched into the village and demanded the guilty party be turned over to him. The Sioux leaders offered to pay for the cow with several prized ponies in an effort to keep the peace. They could not understand the importance placed on one skinny cow, nor could they understand why their offer of payment should be refused.

The young officer became threatening in his demand for the guilty person, and in the melee that followed he and his entire troop were killed. This incident was all the excuse needed for the government to move against the Sioux. In the spring, General Harney and a large expedition marched through the Sioux lands to punish the Sioux whenever and wherever they might be found. On September 3, 1855, General Harney came upon Chief Little Thunder's camp at Ash Hollow, near the emigrant trail. He attacked, and in what must be termed a shameful massacre, killed a hundred and thirty-six of the tribe. The camp was caught between two lines of soldiers, and indicated a willingness to surrender. Their wishes ignored, they fought gallantly to the end.

The white emigrants continued to travel through Sioux country, and the Bozeman trail was established through the very heart of their buffalo country. Attacks continued on wagon trains, and again the Government attempted to resolve matters by a council with Chief Red Cloud and his people. Red Cloud was aware that even as the white government agents talked with him in council, many soldiers were already coming into the area to establish a series of forts along the Bozeman trail. He declared the council a shameful deceit, and vowed to kill every white man found beyond the Powder River. Some of the following battles are often referred to as Red Cloud's War.

The Fetterman Fight, December 21, 1866

A detachment of soldiers under Captain Fetterman went out from Fort Phil Kearny to relieve a wood supply train, and were enticed into a cleverly planned ambush. There were eighty-one soldiers killed, including Captain Fetterman. The Indians, comprised of Sioux and Cheyenne under Red Cloud and Two Moons, lost an undetermined number of warriors,

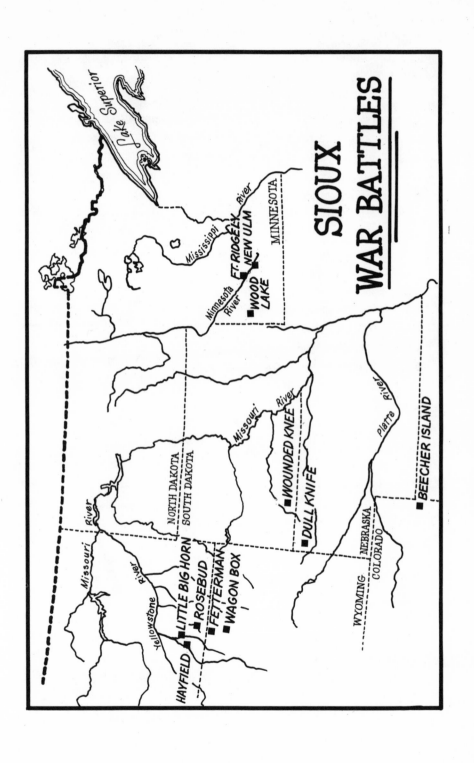

said by Red Cloud at a later time to have been eleven killed and many wounded.

The Hayfield Fight, August 1, 1867

The troops at Fort C. F. Smith, on the Bozeman trail, were equipped with new Springfield rifles capable of firepower unknown to the Sioux at the time. Civilian workers were armed with even better weapons, the Spencer and Henry repeating rifles. A detachment of nineteen soldiers and five civilian workers was dispatched from the fort to cut and lay in a supply of hay for the horses at the fort, and while doing so were attacked by a force of nearly a thousand Sioux and Cheyenne warriors. Failing to lure the workers into an ambush, the Indians attacked the small group time after time.

Fortified behind a corral, and shooting from behind wagons and logs, the small group poured a devastating fire into the attackers, repulsing all attacks, until relief arrived from the fort. Only three of the work detail were killed and four were wounded. Indian losses were hard to determine, since they always removed their dead and wounded from the battlefield, but reports would indicate that fifty to a hundred Sioux and Cheyenne were killed.

The Wagon Box Fight, August 2, 1867

A large force of over fifteen hundred Sioux warriors, led by Red Cloud, attacked a wood supply force near Fort Phil Kearny one day later. Red Cloud was not aware of the previous day's battle nor was he aware of the new rifle power in the hands of the enemy. The results of this battle proved to be every bit as disastrous to the Sioux as had been the case at the Hayfield fight. A group of thirty-two soldiers and civilian workers, firing from a barricade of wagon boxes, successfully repulsed charge after charge of the Sioux, until Red Cloud recalled his forces and moved away.

Indian losses in this encounter have been estimated as high as seven hundred, although a lesser figure of sixty killed and over a hundred wounded may be closer to reality. This fight probably caused the Sioux chiefs to abandon their plans to attack the forts, and from that time on they were reluctant to wage attacks against superior firepower of the Army. Thereafter most fighting was done from a defensive plan, fighting when their people were threatened by advancing Army troops.

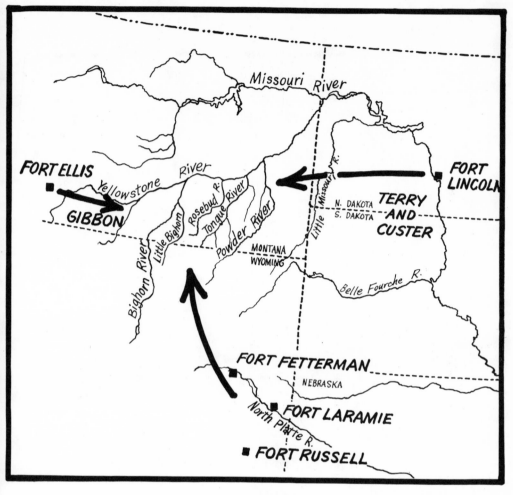

A Major Campaign

A major campaign to crush the Sioux was ordered by General Sheridan from his Chicago headquarters in 1876. The plans called for three columns to converge on the Sioux country. Colonel Gibbon and five hundred men were to march east from Fort Ellis. General Crook was to march north toward the head of Rosebud Creek with a large body of troops. The largest column, over nine hundred men under General Terry, was to march west from Fort Lincoln. The Seventh Cavalry, led by Lieut. Col. (Brevet General) Custer, was in Terry's force.

The approximate location of the Sioux had been established, and a final strategy session was held between Terry, Gibbon and Custer. Noting that the Sioux were probably camped in the Little Bighorn Valley, it was

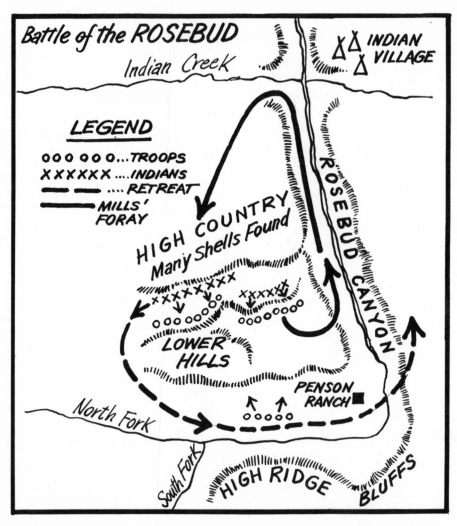

decided that Custer's Seventh Cavalry would go up the Rosebud, cross the mountains and move up the Little Bighorn Valley from the south. Terry would go with Gibbon and come down the Little Bighorn from the north, catching the Sioux between the two forces. Meanwhile, General Crook was operating in the Rosebud area, unknown to Terry and his forces.

The Rosebud Battle, June 17, 1876

General Crook, with a force of over thirteen hundred, was intent on attacking a Sioux encampment rumored to be on the Rosebud. It was here that many tribes had combined for mutual protection. There were both Sioux and Cheyenne in the encampment, and it was here, on about June 10, that a great sun dance was held. The sun dance was directed by Sitting Bull, and he told of his vision that saw all the white soldiers killed. It is believed by many that this sun dance and Sitting Bull's "medicine" instilled great courage and purpose in the assembled tribes.

A few days later, the Indians became aware of Crook's large force nearby. Under cover of night, many warriors moved to surrounding hills near Crook's encampment. On the morning of June 17, they attacked. The battle raged, and instances of hand-to-hand fighting were numerous. The Sioux would charge, fight, quickly withdraw, then charge again in hit-and-run tactics that proved deadly to the soldiers. These tactics were new to the troops since the Indian's style had previously been to stay at a distance and take few chances, unless the situation looked like an easy victory.

It may have been the presence of Sitting Bull and his encouragement that drove the warriors to great heights that day, or it may have been the leadership genius of Crazy Horse that prompted the change in battle tactics, but the effect was a resounding victory for the Sioux. General Crook's forces lost over fifty killed and wounded, and Sioux losses were estimated at eleven killed and five wounded. The results of this battle probably remained fresh in the minds of the Sioux warriors as they went forth to battle with Custer a week later on the Little Bighorn.

The Little Bighorn Battle, June 25, 1876

History has recorded many versions of what transpired on the Little Bighorn, but the ultimate results leave little room for doubt. The companies led by Major Reno and Captain Benteen, in their fight for survival, suffered heavy casualties, and the entire command of Lieut. Col. (General) Custer was killed in what historians portray as Custer's Last Stand. Historians' figures indicate that Reno and Benteen lost 47 killed and 52 wounded, and that Custer's command of 213 men was killed to the last man. Sioux losses have been estimated at less than fifty. Accounts of the battle indicate that the leading battle chiefs for the Sioux were Crazy Horse, Gall, and Crow King, and such Cheyenne chiefs as Two Moons, Little Horse, and White Bull. Sitting Bull, although not participating

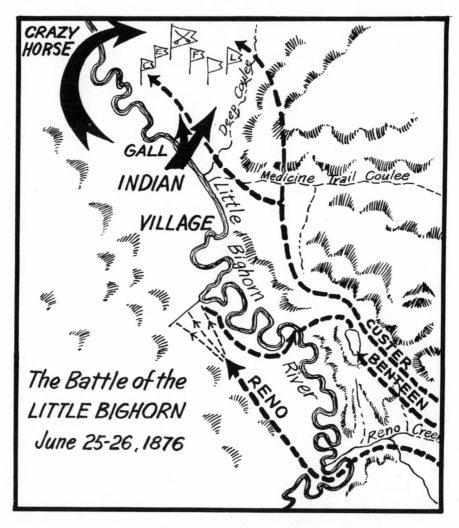

The Battle of the LITTLE BIGHORN June 25-26, 1876

actively in the battle, was there in the role of the great and respected medicine man and may well have been the power behind the strategy of the day.

The Sioux had won their greatest victory in their stand against the onrushing white society, but it was a victory without gain. Following the battle, the tribes scattered to the winds, hunted and hounded unmercifully by the Army. The end was near for the Sioux nation, and with the subsequent massacres of Dull Knife's Cheyenne band at Fort Robinson and of Chief Big Foot's village at Wounded Knee, the bloody campaign closed.

SOME FAMOUS
SIOUX LEADERS

Crazy Horse: A Legend in His Time*

Crazy Horse was born in the period 1841-1844 (records will vary on this date). He was light-complexioned and had light, curly hair as a youth, prompting his people to call him "Curly" or "The light-haired boy." He was the son of Crazy Horse, a holy man of the Oglalas, who later named the boy "His Horse Looking."

In his youth, he had a vision where he saw himself as a solitary leader of his people, one whose duty it was to lead, even if it meant going alone against great odds. In this vision he was given powers that would protect him against harm and told that he was never to attempt to acquire personal wealth or gain. He fashioned his life after this vision and became known as one of great power or "medicine."

While in his teens, he led a war party against a group of enemy Indians and twice charged the enemy by himself, displaying great feats of bravery. Following this exploit, his father gave him his own name of Crazy Horse, after a long line of fathers in their family.

He was shy and displayed no ambition to enter any warrior societies or to acquire wealth through acquiring numbers of horses, as most warriors did. He was often seen going from the camp alone to hunt or to meditate in solitary and these characteristics prompted his people to call him their "Strange Man," a term they used with much respect and admiration. Despite his lack of customary wealth and honor symbols, his fame grew as a great warrior and leader, and in the early 1880s the Sioux, in

---

*To the author's knowledge, no authentic photo was ever taken of this great leader. The author also feels that any illustration that was devised to show this leader would not be a true representation and therefore the reader is left to visualize Crazy Horse in terms of his own interpretation.

their war preparations, held a large council composed of many tribes, to select new and younger chiefs for their crisis. In this council four new chiefs were chosen, among them Crazy Horse, and placed over such other chiefs as Red Cloud and Spotted Tail, causing a great deal of intertribal jealousy.

He had a burning ambition or driving force that seemed to be concerned solely with preserving his people and their land from the white government. He scorned those Indians who would periodically live near the forts to enjoy the gifts and food provided by the soldiers and traders. He burned with indignation at the killing and atrocities suffered by his people at the hands of the white army, and was firmly convinced that his vision had provided a meaning to his life. He carried a deep and bitter hostility against the enemy, and every killing, atrocity or broken promise was cataloged into his memory. These feelings cried out to him for revenge, and through his fearless, gallant leadership the name of Crazy Horse became a name to be feared among the people of the frontier, and a name to be revered among the Sioux.

His battle exploits are legendary and his leadership was evident in General Crook's defeat at the Rosebud and in Custer's humiliating annihilation at the Little Bighorn.

As the Sioux resistance finally died out and the suffering of his people increased, he led them onto the reservation, where he attempted to live in peace.

Many other reservation chiefs, Red Cloud and Spotted Tail among them, jealous of his great popularity and ambitious for reservation power of their own, attempted to discredit Crazy Horse in many ways. Through their influence and through false rumors that he was planning to go on the warpath again, he was placed under arrest through trickery, and killed while resisting, at Fort Robinson on September 5, 1877.

The life of perhaps the greatest of all the Sioux leaders was taken, as it had existed, amidst the turmoil of cultures in conflict.

His last words, spoken near death, were, ". . . tell the people it is no use to depend on me any more . . ."

Sitting Bull: Great Medicine Maker

Sitting Bull was a noted warrior and tribal leader of the Hunkpapa Sioux. He was born in the South Dakota area about 1834, and was named "Jumping Badger" as a boy.

He showed great skill as a hunter while only ten years of age, and by fourteen, he accompanied his father, a chief, on a raid against the Crows, where he scored his first "coup." The tribe honored him for this feat, and as his honors grew so did his ability to make "medicine" through his visions. His name was changed to Sitting Bull, meaning, in effect, that a "sacred buffalo bull is among us." Few names were ever given relating to the buffalo, held sacred by the Sioux, indicating the high regard the people had for his accomplishments.

He became very influential, and many bands looked to him for a form of leadership, although he was not in the true sense a chief.

Sitting Bull took an active part in the plains wars of the 1860s, and personally led a raid on Fort Buford in 1866. He was continually leading raids against the Crow and Shoshoni tribes, driving them from the Sioux buffalo country.

He refused to live on a reservation and scorned all Indians who did so. Instead, he continued to stay away from the white men as much as possible, leading his people in search of the buffalo.

His refusal to go onto the reservation was one reason that prompted the U. S. Government to wage military war against the Sioux in the campaign of 1876.

It was during this campaign that Sitting Bull conducted a sun dance just before the historic battle of the Little Bighorn. At this gathering, attended by bands of many tribes, he inspired the people with his vision

in which he saw many white soldiers killed by the Sioux. This "medicine" is thought to have instilled the Sioux with renewed spirit and determination to resist the white army, and may have been very instrumental in the outcome of the Little Bighorn battle, where, as he had predicted, all the white soldiers were killed.

Following the Little Bighorn battle, the tribes scattered to the winds and Sitting Bull led his followers to Canada to escape the searching Army troops. Hunger and hardships forced him back into the United States, and he and his band surrendered at Fort Buford in 1881.

Sitting Bull lived on the reservation from that time on, although still not taking up the white man's ways, and this rebellious attitude caused the reservation agents to attempt to discredit him whenever possible in the eyes of his people.

The Ghost Dance movement began in 1890, and Sitting Bull encouraged it. The Government officials hastily concluded that he was stirring up the Sioux for war, and he was arrested and killed while resisting his captors on December 15, 1890.

Sitting Bull could have become a chief through tribal inheritance, since his father was a chief, but he gained his fame through his ability to organize and as a "holy man" among his people.

Red Cloud: Warrior, Statesman
and Politician

Red Cloud was once a principal chief of the Oglala Sioux and perhaps one of the most famous and powerful chiefs of his time.

His name is said to have come from the way in which his scarlet-blanketed warriors covered the hillsides like a red cloud.

He was born in the Platte River country, into the "Snake" family, one of the most powerful families of the tribe. He rose to power through the force of his character and through crafty tribal politics.

His father was rumored to have died as a result of the white man's whisky, and the young warrior and chief became a leader of Indian resistance to the white man's intrusion into buffalo country. Many of the battles fought in the 1860s were thought of as Red Cloud's War, since he was one of the main figures at that time.

In his youth, Red Cloud ranked high as a respected warrior and counted some eighty "coups" in his fighting days. Later he directed military campaigns much as a general, and represented the Sioux as a treaty chief at the Fort Laramie Treaty of 1868. In this treaty, he won many concessions from the United States Government and became highly respected by his followers as one who had beaten the white man at his own game, that of making treaties.

Following the treaty of 1868, Red Cloud seems to have given up all thoughts of war and lived a peaceful reservation life in which he attempted to gain favor with the Government authorities. He was getting along in years by this time and in poor health. Leadership of the Oglalas had passed to Crazy Horse, causing him to feel bitter and jealous, ultimately leading

him to contribute to the discrediting and death of Crazy Horse in 1877. These reasons may have caused him to give up the warpath. It may have been, too, that he saw the futility of leading his people further into a conflict that he saw little chance of winning.

Red Cloud will long be remembered as a warrior, a chief, a statesman and, above all, a crafty tribal political force.

Gall: Great Military Leader

Gall was a leading war chief of the Hunkpapa tribe. He was noted as a brave, fearless warrior in his youth, and became a war chief leader noted for his military genius and ability to lead.

He was instrumental in leading the Sioux to victory at the Little Bighorn, and after that battle, he and his followers went with Sitting Bull into Canada to escape the army of the United States.

Life in Canada was full of hardships and food scarce, and in January of 1881 he led his band to surrender at Poplar River, Montana.

He settled as a farmer on the Standing Rock reservation in the Dakotas and became friendly to the white Government officials. He was appointed an Indian court judge in 1889, and in his later years he was known to denounce Sitting Bull and his leadership abilities. This change in belief is thought to have been influenced by pressures and favors from the white Government officials in their attempts to discredit Sitting Bull in the eyes of his people.

Little Crow: From Peace to War

Little Crow was the main chief of the Kaposia tribe of Mdewakanton Sioux, living near the junction of the Minnesota and Mississippi rivers. For many years he lived in peace among the white settlers and was a principal signer of the Mendota Treaty of 1851.

The failure of the Government to live up to its treaty agreements was one major reason that caused him to eventually go to war against the white people.

He led his people in the Sioux Uprising of 1862, in which the Minnesota frontier ran red with the blood of over a thousand white settlers and soldiers.

He was defeated at the Battle of Wood Lake and fled with his followers to the north and west. Many of his warriors captured in this short war were hanged at a mass execution at Mankato, Minnesota, in December of 1862, and there are many historians who feel that the results of this war did much to inflame the actions of the Western Sioux in the following years.

In 1863, Little Crow was killed by a farmer near Hutchinson, Minnesota. It was rumored that he and his son had come down into Minnesota from Canada on a horse-stealing raid.

Little Crow will long be remembered as a leader who tried to live at peace with the white settlers and when he became disillusioned by continued failures on the part of the Government to deal fairly with his people, made a difficult decision to lead his people in a war to regain their lost lands.

ah Ko wah mu ne

shades walking

the Crow or Petit Corbeau

Sioux camp July 2 1851

Rain in the Face: Warrior

Rain in the Face was a noted warrior of the Hunkpapa tribe, gaining his fame not through inheritance, but because of his many brave deeds.

He was a leader in the Fetterman battle in 1866, and was a leading participant in the Custer fight at the Little Bighorn. It was rumored that he was the one who had killed Custer in that battle, and for many years this story was told. Later study of the battle and of accounts of all who participated proved the story untrue.

He fled to Canada with Sitting Bull after the Custer battle and later returned to surrender at Fort Keogh, Montana, in 1880, and from that time on lived on a reservation.

Kicking Bear: Ghost Dance Promoter

Kicking Bear was a noted medicine man or holy man of the Sioux. He gained much notoriety as a leader or promoter of the Ghost Dance movement in 1890. He organized the first ghost dance in the Upper Midwest, held at Sitting Bull's camp on the Standing Rock reservation.

He was labeled a "hostile," and the white Government officials thought he was stirring up the Sioux for another war and had him arrested and imprisoned for a time.

Appendix

SUGGESTED BIBLIOGRAPHY FOR FURTHER READING

Crazy Horse: The Strange Man of the Oglalas, by Sandoz.
Black Elk Speaks: Being the Life Story of a Holy Man of the Sioux, by Neihardt.
Warpath and Bivouac, by Finerty.
Wooden Leg: A Warrior Who Fought Custer, by Marquis.
(The above books are Bison Books, published by the University of Nebraska Press.)
The Dakota or Sioux, Gopher Historian Leaflet Series No. 5, by Minnesota Historical Society.
Red Cloud, by McGaa.
These Were the Sioux, by Sandoz.
Sitting Bull, Champion of the Sioux, by Vestal.
Bury My Heart at Wounded Knee, by Brown.
Gifts From the Indians, Gopher Historian Pamphlet No. 3, Minnesota Historical Society.

CULTURE VOCABULARY

The following words are listed to strengthen your vocabulary in reading about the Sioux. Some are Sioux words, some are of other language derivation, but all are used extensively in materials written by and of the Sioux.

Akicita—Warrior societies of the Sioux.
Breechcloth—Cloth or skin garment worn about the midsection.
Coup—To strike a living or dead enemy.

Echa!—Meaning "well done."

Holy Man—Medicine man or "shaman," one capable of having visions and making power or "medicine" for the people.

Hoye!—A sound of agreement meaning "yes."

Hou!—A sound of approval or agreement.

Hou, cola!—Meaning "greetings, friend."

Hoka hey!—A war cry meaning "to charge."

Yi-hoo!—A cry of the hunter after killing a buffalo.

Hoppo!—A cry meaning "let's go!"

Hetchetu aloh!—Meaning "it is so or it is the truth."

Heyokas—The thunder dreamers, a special ceremonial group that conducted ceremonials in which everything was done backwards to please the great spirits in times when things were not going well or to cheer the people in such times.

Medicine—Special power provided by medicine men or by individuals through visions or sacred actions.

Massacre—Killing inflicted on helpless people usually not able to fight back or not willing to resist.

Minne—Meaning "water."

Minnetanka—Meaning "big water."

Minnesota—Meaning "cloudy water."

Pemmican—Dried, pounded buffalo meat mixed with hot tallow and stored in skin bags for future use.

Parfleches—Skin bags in which pemmican was stored.

Paha sapa—Meaning "black hills."

Tanka—Meaning "big or great."

Tepeetanka—Meaning "big house."

Travois—Pole and skin device pulled by ponies or dogs, used to carry things from one campsite to another.

Tepee—Skin-covered structure supported by cedar poles.

Vision—Dream or mental image received while under stress of fasting or under extreme pain.

Waga chun—The sacred cottonwood tree used in the sun dance.

Wakan—Spirit, mysterious or sacred.

Wakantanka—Meaning "Great Spirit."

Wakantepee—Meaning "spirit house or church."

Wasichus—Meaning "the white people."

Wanekia—One who makes live, son of the Great Spirit.

Wasna—Another name for pemmican, usually mixed with berries for added flavor.

Wickiup—Small willow pole shelter covered with skins or robes, usually accommodating from one to four people.

MEASURING TIME: MOONS AND MONTHS

The names of the Plains Indian moons and your own months of the year are given below. Note that the Indian moons are named to designate times of the year with meaning related to the natural environment and its relationship to the Indian, while the calendar you are familiar with has the months named after Roman gods and Roman persons and other words from the Roman (Latin) language.

Which seems to be the better system of naming these units of time in your opinion?

Plains Indian Moons	*The Gregorian Months*
Moon of Frost in the Tepee.	January, for the god Janus.
Moon of the Dark-Red Calves.	February, from Februarius, feast of purification.
Moon of the Snowblind.	March, for the god Mars.
Moon of Red Grass Appearing.	April, for the goddess Aphrodite.
Moon When the Ponies Shed.	May, for the goddess Malus.
Moon of Making Fat.	June, for Junius, Italian goddess.
Moon of the Red Cherries.	July, for Julius Caesar.
Moon When Cherries Turn Black.	August, for Augustus Caesar.
Moon When the Calves Grow Hair.	September, from Latin number septum.
Moon When Plums Are Scarlet.	October, from Latin number octo.
Moon of the Falling Leaves.	November, from Latin number novem.
Moon of the Popping Trees.	December, from Latin number decem.

INDIAN SIGN LANGUAGE

A problem of communicating between tribes speaking different languages or dialects was common among American Indians, and when language failed, a system of signs, gestures and symbols was used to convey a message.

Early fur traders and explorers found this language of signs a convenient way to talk with the Indians, and soon this language system became a widely accepted means of communication throughout the frontier regions.

Some examples are given to show how sign language worked. You can probably add several more examples of your own, and be assured that your suggestions were probably used if they measure up to the requirement of "getting the message across."

Example 1—Holding out an empty hand, palm side to the person addressed meant, "I come as a friend. No weapon is in my hand."

Example 2—Holding one finger to the lips meant, "Be quiet." (Have you ever used this sign?)

Example 3—Holding cupped hand to the ear meant, "I cannot hear you" or "Listen."

Example 4—A motion or beckoning gesture meant, "Come," or "Follow me."

Example 5—Closing the eyes and holding the head to one side, resting on the hands, meant, "I am sleepy or tired," or this sign followed by pointing to a person might mean, "Are you sleepy or tired?"

Example 6—Rubbing the stomach and pointing to the mouth meant, "I am hungry," or "Can you give me food?"

Example 7—Holding one hand high above the head meant, "Silence," or "Attention please."

Example 8—Passing the side or edge of the hand across the throat meant, "I have killed," or "I will kill."

Example 9—offering a peace pipe and a war club or arrow to another meant, "Make your choice, war or peace," or "Will you choose peace or war?"

Example 10—These written symbols might have meant, "We jour-
neyed from this river to the other river. The journey took three suns
(days) or three sleeps."

Example 11—Sometimes a person might indicate his name by using
a symbol such as the following, which meant, "My name is Black Elk."

Index